Helping Hands

Helping Hands

Volunteer Work in Education

By

Gayle Janowitz

THE UNIVERSITY OF CHICAGO PRESS

Chicago and London

This book is also available in a clothbound edition from

THE UNIVERSITY OF CHICAGO PRESS, CHICAGO & LONDON
The University of Toronto Press, Toronto 5, Canada

Second Impression 1966
Printed in the United States of America

Preface

In October, 1962, I began to work with volunteers in tutoring and homework help at the Hyde Park Neighborhood Club Study Center of Chicago. My work with Bruno Bettelheim at the Sonia Shankman Orthogenic School had given me an orientation which I felt was applicable in helping underachieving children. Although these children do not have emotional disturbances, they are beginning to feel discouraged in school. I believed that such youngsters would also respond to Bettelheim's philosophy which is built on respect for the individual. It was on the basis of my interpretation of his teachings rather than from courses or textbooks in remedial reading that I learned what I consider a valid orientation toward all children, including those from economically depressed backgrounds who need academic help. In a brief pamphlet entitled *After-School Study Centers: Volunteer Work in Reading*, I wrote my limited observations on the problems and potentialities for supplementary educational efforts.

Since 1962, the volunteer movement in education has spread rapidly throughout the country. Enthusiasm, determination, and a desire to innovate have been the most dramatic aspects of this outburst of activity. This was all to the good, but experienced guidance for such efforts was limited and relevant materials almost non-existent. In October, 1964, I started a three-year demonstration and evaluation program with the support of the U.S. Office of Education in order to help improve our understanding of the problems of academic achievement and the role of the volunteer in education.

Although this research is still in progress, I decided to record the available information, as well as our experiences, because of the increasing interest in volunteer work. This report must therefore be considered an interim document while we collect more experiences and discover which of our efforts are effective and rewarding.

Since this book was supported in part by a federal grant, royalties will be used to enable students to do collaborative studies to help improve public education.

GAYLE JANOWITZ

Department of Political and Social Science
Illinois Institute of Technology

Contents

Introduction

In his last speech on education, which was, in fact, the last public address he made in Washington before leaving for Texas, President Kennedy remarked that in education, "things don't just happen; they are made to happen." Gayle Janowitz's work with volunteers in education is a wonderful example of the reality of this observation. So often, in the past, we have seen what almost amounts to apathy develop in our view of what can be done to insure quality education for all children. Today, with growing frequency, we begin to see bursts of unbridled and often incautious enthusiasm surround untested innovations in education, particularly in programs for children who need help. Mrs. Janowitz's well-documented and carefully evaluated experience with volunteer work in education offers a welcome "let's take time to take a look" approach in this major area of social concern.

Public interest and involvement in volunteer work in education is not new. In fact, the informal education of many primitive societies is much more akin to such an approach than it is to our own highly structured system of formal education. What is new is the use to which we would put such work. Growing out of the civil rights movement and the war on poverty, and closely associated with new hopes for cognitive intervention in early childhood, these volunteer programs are expected to compensate for the inequalities in educational opportunity that remain a part of the American school system. This is an important and valid use for volunteer work and tutoring and many of us applaud the shift away from apathy and inactivity. But we must make certain that enthusiasm is joined with evaluation and good will is tempered by good judgment. Creatively developed and properly used, such programs can increase the academic performance and social competency of children in ways that most present-day schools cannot. But they should supplement rather than subvert what the child learns in the school.

Ultimately, the case for successful out-of-school programs rests on the proposition that they do make a difference in the lives of children who have been exposed to them. Until now, those who have been involved in administering such programs have been little troubled by any systematic appraisal of their effects. If anything, there has been a wonderful, childlike optimism about their success. Now, faced with the urgency of the demands we are about to place on programs which supplement formal education — pre-school learning laboratories, community art and science centers and tutoring programs provided by a multitude of agencies, public and private, religious and secular, national and local — we are casting about for answers that tell if, how, and why such programs work. Some means must be developed to train the inspired amateur to make the best use of his enthusiasm, to measure how effective various types of programs are with different types of children, and to make this information readily available to those who need it. Gayle Janowitz's work is a first and significant step to seeing that this is made to happen.

Francis A. J. Ianni
Washington, D.C.

1

Growth of Volunteer Work

One of the major social concerns in the United States is to close
the gap in quality between suburban schools and those of the
inner city. Inner city areas have a variety of problems such as
tremendous population pressure, overcrowded schools, and out-
moded buildings. Schools in the inner city have not been supported financially to the same extent as those in the suburbs.
Teacher and pupil turnover both may be high and therefore
very disruptive to school achievement. Thus, such schools are
especially in need of new approaches to solve their academic
problems.

Academic underachievement is one measure of our school
problems, and it is conservatively estimated at about 30 per cent
of the national school population. Although there is no evidence
that underachievement is greater than ever before, the number
of children involved is very large. Because of automation, available jobs for unskilled people are decreasing, and underachievement is therefore more of a problem.

Underachievement is not a new problem to the schools. In
1909, Leonard Ayres wrote in *Laggards in Our Schools*[1] that
on the basis of school records, reports, and statistics published
by government agencies, "about 33 per cent of all pupils in public
schools" were retarded in their academic progress.

[1] Leonard Ayres, *Laggards in Our Schools* (New York, 1909), p. 3.

A generation ago young people left school and went to work. They were called school-leavers. Now such youngsters are called dropouts because there are no jobs for them. In the last three decades, the percentage of youngsters finishing high school has gone up steadily. Approximately 70 per cent of American young people now complete high school, but it is among the 30 per cent who do not graduate that the greatest difficulty in entering the job market is found. They are concentrated in the inner city, and the continued trends of urbanization and automation indicate that the problems of inner city schools will remain the greatest challenge to mass education.

Volunteer work in education has as its special objective helping city children from low-income and poverty backgrounds. These are primarily the Negro, Puerto Rican, and Mexican youngsters. There are also many second or third generation families of European background as well as southern Appalachian families whose children need assistance in their school work.

But it would be an error to believe that those who need help are limited to the inner city, although they clearly are concentrated there. Pockets of poverty and low income are to be found in suburban areas of every metropolitan center of the United States. In rural areas the need is also extensive. It is not true, moreover, that underachievement is exclusively a matter of low-income families. In every school there are groups of children who, because of a lack of appropriate family encouragement or for a variety of other reasons, fail to measure up to their potentials and who need the individual attention that volunteer work can offer.

Although basic solutions will have to come from the state legislatures and the federal government, efforts to develop compensatory education by the use of volunteers have developed and increased rapidly during the last several years. For years schools have used volunteers for many non-academic functions. In recent years they have begun to develop academic programs using volunteers. Many of these involve tutoring — individual help given by an adult to a child in the classroom or in any room available in the school during school hours. Some of these programs are operated by independent citizens' groups working in cooperation with the schools; others are developed by the schools themselves. In addition, some public schools have begun to use volunteers after school for homework help or individual tutoring. In some communities, after-school help developed first because this was the only time that volunteers could be used in school facilities.

Complementing the efforts of schools, many voluntary organizations have developed academic programs outside of the school to help children. These volunteer efforts of community organizations, civic associations, and churches are often called after-school study centers. For example, in Chicago a great deal of work has gone into after-school programs. The efforts of college students and housewives, as well as employed and retired adults, resulted in a number of tutoring projects and after-school centers. Many other groups wanted to start projects, and it became necessary for them to have professional help. The Human Relations Commission, an official agency of the City of Chicago, began to work with these groups. It gave conferences for the directors of projects and periodically published a continuing directory of their locations. It also organized a staff of four full-time members to engage in community organization and technical assistance. By 1965, after three years, there were more than 150 centers in the city of Chicago helping grade school and high school children and adults. These centers are highly diversified in their programs, reflecting the needs and resources of individual local communities.

The growth of volunteer work in education in Chicago is typical of what has happened throughout the country. Tutoring projects and after-school centers are developing in most major cities and in many suburban communities. Some operate in school buildings; others in storefronts, settlement houses, churches, boys' clubs, and the like. An after-school study center is a workshop for children where they can improve their academic skills and have an opportunity for social intercourse under the supervision of interested adults. A report issued by the National School Volunteer Program, Public Education Association in April, 1965, showed that of the public school systems of the fourteen largest cities, exclusive of New York City, ten made use of volunteers. Citizens' groups were important in the recruitment of these volunteers.

The advantage of using school buildings is that they become more of a community center in the eyes of the local residents. The tax-supported facilities are available, and a sponsoring group does not have to use energy and money to develop a new location. It is true that for some children it seems important to walk away from the school building and enter a new setting, but for just as many other children it is meaningful to have a study center in their own school. If the school can benefit from the prestige and genuine appreciation of the community for a good service, it helps to bring the school closer to the whole community.

After-school study centers and tutoring projects are examples of compensatory education — those attempts to help the school succeed in its basic task of giving each child an education that is meaningful to him and will prepare him for some acceptable role in the future. No educational system will ever achieve complete success with all children. The waste of human talent that present levels of achievement represent, however, is just not compatible with the urbanized and mechanized society that we have and will continue to develop.

There is widespread interest in both remedial efforts and preschool work. Neither of these approaches, however, can be expected to solve problems that are basic to the school system itself. Inner city schools must have financial support at least as adequate as suburban schools have. New or improved facilities and more teachers are needed. Teachers ought to be relieved of housekeeping chores and paper work so that they can devote more time to teaching. Training of teachers should continually improve, especially in-service training, in order to help them overcome their own prejudices and misconceptions about inner city children. In addition, other innovations include more exciting teaching materials, the use of community people with special talents, and more flexible procedures to allow the student to proceed at his own pace. These changes will help children succeed more often and will help teachers to let them succeed.

Therefore both remedial and preschool efforts must be supported, but they cannot be considered the answer to all — or even most — of our educational problems. Both approaches have become popular, however, and unfortunately there is a danger that they will become gimmicks which will distract attention from the whole range of educational problems. Preschool centers are obviously needed, and they should be an effective device for helping children, but only if they are integrated in a meaningful way with the rest of our school system.

Tutoring projects and study centers may also suffer from their newly won popularity. The many volunteers being recruited are often given the impression that they are going to make a major contribution in the life of a child. Most of them will not. Volunteers can make a small, but meaningful, contribution, and they can learn a good deal. They are neither as important as some ardent recruiters would wish them to be, nor are they to be dismissed as temporary do-gooders.

These two major efforts in compensatory education share other problems besides their popularity. Both must avoid being viewed as punitive measures. To tell parents who are often as deprived as their children that society is going to fix up their children and make them respectable can only make these parents more hostile. Obviously, the families cannot do the job alone, but the help given them either can be a co-operative experience or it can be an expression of an attitude that someone with superior skills will do something for someone of assumed inferior ability. To force the participation of parents is to manipulate people. It is only necessary to accept their need to share in the education of their children. With this basic attitude, opportunities for sincere cooperation may be found. Genuine parental involvement may develop, as it has in some school systems.

The need for both preschool and remedial programs has provided excuses for some educators to explain the failure of their schools. Educators have said that their job is impossible because they did not reach the children young enough, and because there are too many deprived children. Teachers use such labels as "disadvantaged" to explain their lack of success. What will happen if great hopes are placed on remedial or preschool help, only to find that their success is limited because basic changes needed in the schools are ignored?

The richness of educational opportunities in America should not be limited to an age group or to one approach. There must be opportunities for all ages, a number of second chances, and a variety of remedial programs. Most responsible leaders agree that the only real error we can make is inaction. The only hope for reaching the children who need help is for thousands of people to become concerned enough to try. The very fact that so many volunteers are willing to become involved is a healthy sign. Despite what some experts say, enough people do not believe that these children are lost because they were not helped earlier or that they are hopeless because of their assumed defects. Enough people are convinced that if these children are approached with the same respect and consideration shown to any other child, they will in fact relate to volunteers and accept their help.

Academic programs using volunteers have become part of the war on poverty to help prevent dropouts. The majority of school dropouts have failed at least one grade early in school. They achieve poorly in school and lack good work habits and job experience. By the time they drop out, the traditional academic program or after-school center cannot hope to reverse years of a trend toward failure. It is impressive how hopeful elementary school children are, despite their difficulties in school. These third- through sixth-graders who come in large numbers to after-school centers are still full of hope and expectations despite their low reading scores and poor grades. If they can be reached when they are just beginning to feel defeated — and before they have given up — there should be less need in later years for more expensive and elaborate remedial efforts.

Work-study programs are required for those youngsters who are older and closer to becoming dropouts. Unfortunately, a lengthening of compulsory education is sometimes suggested. By the time these children reach high school the years of failure have already taken their toll. Forcing the schools to keep them is not only punitive to the children but to the schools as well. The whole school suffers because the subject-oriented training of high school teachers makes it difficult to develop a remedial program for low achievers. Instead, effort is required to expand work-study programs which give these youngsters meaningful academic help and work experiences. Since this job cannot be done by the schools alone, private industries and volunteer agencies are being asked to help.

Another reason that study centers and tutoring projects have become part of the war on poverty is that they represent a genuine grass roots movement of interested citizens. The fact that high school and college students, housewives, professionals, and retired men and women are volunteering by the thousands means that there is an enormous reserve of good will and labor available. It also means that academic help for children is a cause which has wide appeal. It is impressive that women who cannot afford to hire a sitter exchange baby-sitting in order to give an afternoon a week to a center. Many volunteers have been working in projects for as long as three years and expect to continue.

Volunteer work has always been a tradition in America. The new aspect of this work is that volunteers have become interested in education because of increased awareness of the inequalities in educational opportunity. The job to be done is so great that the need for these people will continue for years.

II

Organization of a Study Center

GOALS

The goal of volunteer work in education is to increase the academic competence and the self-respect of children who need help. These two needs of the children are so interwoven that a contribution to one reinforces the other. We know that children underachieve because they are not able to show what they can do or to use the ability they have. They do not have the academic skills other children their age have, so their self-respect suffers. Although we are always aware that our job is to improve both skills and attitudes, we know that helping in either area helps in the other.

An after-school study center or tutoring project has these specific goals:

1. To help improve academic achievement in school children, especially in reading and arithmetic.

2. To help develop more positive attitudes toward school and academic achievement.

3. To demonstrate to youngsters that learning, discussion, and reading are valid leisure-time activities.

4. To develop approaches for reaching the families of the youngsters who are being served.

5. To give volunteers a chance to make a useful contribution.

Just as it is the responsibility of parents of grade-school children to see that their children do their homework and to support their schools while working for better education, so it is the responsibility of volunteers to support the schools and teachers. Their job is to help children succeed in school.

In some communities the same center can be used by a variety of age groups. During the school day an after-school center may be a suitable setting for preschool care. If the center is used only in the afternoons for elementary school children, the same facilities might be used in the evenings for a high school program or for adult education.

The quality of any program will depend upon:

1. Definition of goals and groups to be served. Volunteer work in education has spread so rapidly with so few clear-cut models that groups have tended to take over a program without defining their own needs and resources. One example of this is the first study center in a midwestern city which opened for children from grades one through eight from several neighborhood schools. Because of the wide publicity about this center, many other programs started the same way. Generally, they were overwhelmed with numbers of children. They overlooked the fact that first- and second-graders do not have homework and cannot be expected to use a library setting for long hours. Some centers have had to redefine their program and thus disappoint many children. Volunteers were also disappointed if recruited for a specific job, such as individual help with children, only to find that the number of children was too great for such work.

Homework help and tutoring are defined as two different but highly related services performed by volunteers. Homework help is the encouragement and assistance that an adult gives to a group of youngsters in coping with their regular classroom assignments. It is the kind of assistance that an educated middle-class parent extends to his children, which is unfortunately often missing in the culture of poverty.

Tutoring is more intensive assistance to children to overcome deficiencies in classroom performance, especially in reading and arithmetic. It involves one volunteer tutor and one pupil who meet regularly to work on supplementary assignments and with special materials. It is designed both to assist motivation by direct and immediate interpersonal support and to give remedial help in basic academic skills. Although most volunteer work in education is called tutoring, the major part is limited to homework help, but on a one-to-one basis. The use of the term tutoring is unfortunate, for in some neighborhoods it apparently has frightened away potential volunteers.

Homework help can more easily be developed, since it requires less training and supervision, and one adult can help several children. Tutoring can be done by non-professionals but needs professional guidance, either volunteer or paid. Specific age groups and functions should be identified in the beginning, and the scope should be rather limited because most centers have the experience of being overwhelmed at first with children who want help. Since in poor neighborhoods children tend to come to the centers as a family or group, however, flexibility of procedure is necessary. Natural groupings need to be accepted and strengthened. The concept of specific age groups coming at specific hours is not rigidly applicable in poor neighborhoods because older siblings are so often responsible for younger children.

2. Strength of leadership. A project needs a strong enough leadership core to insure continuing operation. After-school centers usually require one part-time paid co-ordinator.

3. Handling of volunteers. Volunteers need supervision, recognition of their contribution, and some feeling of "esprit de corps." Having resource people available, holding informal meetings after the sessions with the children and periodic discussion meetings, or having luncheons with outside speakers are all useful methods for maintaining group support.

4. Relations with schools. Initial and continuing cooperation with the schools is important. Schools are a crucial source of both referrals and evaluation.

Our educational system assumes that basic skills of reading are mastered by the end of the third grade. Teachers of fourth grade level and beyond are expected to develop and concentrate on more advanced reading skills. Actually, large numbers of children do not achieve adequately in reading, although reading is basic for later success in school. Such children are often not identified as retarded readers until they fall two full academic years behind in reading. Then they may be put on a waiting list for a reading clinic. By this time they are often in the upper grades and have suffered years of underachievement.

There is evidence that a one-to-one relationship between a pupil and a volunteer is useful in helping to motivate and to give these children the skills that they need. A volunteer is in a position to motivate and support a child who is beginning to feel defeated in the classroom situation. A tutor can find or develop individual interests because he has the time that the classroom teacher does not have. Because of the great amount of personal attention required, this job can never be done by professionals.

There seems to be in every school a large number of normally intelligent children who are achieving from six months to two years behind their academic level. If these children are referred by schools, they can be helped by volunteers. Non-readers and children more than two years behind may present special problems. In fact, the majority of children referred to volunteer centers are retarded about one to two years in reading. They have proved much more reachable by volunteer efforts than those who are several years behind. Most study centers deal with grade school children, but the approach is being extended to high-school age groups. Study centers do not work with severely disturbed or mentally deficient children.

Homework help has become an accepted part of school achievement. Many children do not have adequate space, proper atmosphere, or adult help in doing their homework. Access to books is a problem for these children. In poor neighborhoods, they are often not allowed to take their school books home, and public libraries often seem cold and hostile. There are no books and magazines in the home, and learning is strictly a school activity.

These needs of children, especially children of the inner city, have led to a recent and expanding development of volunteer efforts to give academic help, both during and after school hours. These two approaches support each other. Younger children can particularly benefit from individual help during school hours, since they are often tired by the end of the school day. The appeal of a new setting in a physically separate facility or with a new staff has resulted in the continual expansion of present after-school centers and the realization that there remains an even greater unfilled need.

Any group wishing to develop an academic after-school program should inform the local schools of its plans and intentions. Public libraries should be approached, since they can often be influenced to help supply resources. Human relations groups, youth welfare commissions, elected officials, church and civic groups, and high school groups (such as clubs for future teachers) should be contacted. Many colleges and universities now have tutoring projects which involve their students. Business concerns and service clubs also have become interested in after-school study centers. Of course, efforts must be made to locate, stimulate, and develop personnel and talent within the community which the study center serves.

PROGRAM

A study center should include: (1) library facilities (either a public library collection or donated books), (2) homework help, and/or (3) individual tutoring. It is not necessary to offer all of these services to have an effective program. Some centers offer only homework help; others offer only tutoring. The site may or may not include library facilities, depending upon the availability of public libraries and books. Close cooperation with the schools is necessary in all cases.

Other facilities that are often added as part of the program include: (1) a paperback bookstore, (2) reading and discussion groups, and (3) a variety of special interest groups (depending upon available volunteer talent). Story-telling hours are frequently built in as a regular activity or as a special activity using trained story-tellers on a volunteer basis. Study centers can also become involved in organizing trips to museums and cultural events.

1. LIBRARY

The location of public libraries is important. If a library is close at hand, many centers arrange to use these facilities at regular intervals and have volunteers escort the children there. (Parents who are reluctant or unable to give academic help are often willing to escort small groups to a library or home from a center after dark.) Centers located at a distance from public libraries often receive, on a loan basis, collections from a public library, or use bookmobiles, or collect donated books. Donated books can be solicited from individuals, schools, and libraries.

Since study centers are mainly volunteer operations, a simple system of marking and distributing books is desirable. The name of the center can be written in the books, and a small white card prepared for each child. The cards may be kept in a recipe box, filed by the last name of the child. Children like to have a list of the books each one has read. In some centers a similar file is used, but the card shows the name of the book and the author and is filed by the book title. When a child takes out a book, his name is written on the card, and it is crossed out when the book is returned. The books, with labels, can be arranged on the shelves by categories so that both children and volunteers can help to keep them in order.

Children should have both easy access to books and help in selecting them. There should be no emphasis on proper reading level. Most of these children have not had very much contact with books, and many like to read below their level. Some also feel compelled to take books which are too difficult for them. A great deal of individual freedom is important. If possible, some books and magazines ought to be available to sell to the children very inexpensively or to give to them so that books and magazines can become more a part of their everyday lives.

2. HOMEWORK HELP

Homework help requires approximately one adult for every five to eight children. Any parent who has a sympathetic understanding of children and the equivalent of a high school education can be useful in homework help. Homework help requires an informal atmosphere which permits the children to talk, to help one another, and to move about.

3. TUTORING PROGRAM

A tutoring program requires some supervision, some minimum record-keeping, and when possible, some professional consultation. The success of tutoring seems to require a one-to-one relationship. Some projects have found that when the adult tried to work with two or three children at a time, attendance dropped off markedly. In those centers where the same group was able to maintain a one-to-one relationship, they were much more successful in keeping the children interested.

4. SPECIAL ACTIVITIES

a) A paperback bookstore can be included in almost any setting. Companies supply a wide selection of paperback books for sale in study centers. In some cities, a local agent handles the distribution of paperbacks. The bookstore can be in a small space and can be available on a once-a-week basis. Some centers also use paperback books to circulate or for use in reading groups.

b) Reading clubs and discussion groups offer an opportunity for children who may not need tutoring to read and discuss. Although designed for good readers, it has been found that some retarded readers more easily join a club than ask for individual help. Often they are later able to accept individual help.

c) Special interest groups in such subjects as mathematics (either remedial or enrichment) or a foreign language can be a part of a study center program. Special activities for all the children are sometimes offered once a week or for holidays, such as puppet shows, musical performances, or art demonstrations. These can be educational, recreational, or both. The emphasis should be on the interest — and therefore the participation — that a program can develop. Active participation by the children is also better than passive watching.

ORGANIZATION AND STAFF

After-school study centers can be organized by school systems or by community organizations. In the development of the use of school facilities after school, the gymnasium has often been the first room to be made available. Libraries and study rooms are equally needed by the children.

The schools have successfully run social centers and are making progress in after-school academic programs. Children have had no conflict in understanding the difference between the social center and the school-room atmosphere. Similarly, they can recognize the difference between the classroom atmosphere and the greater informality of an after-school study center. Although there is a danger that school-based study centers will be viewed as another hour of classroom work, the same problem is faced by every other group sponsoring a study center or tutoring project and can be handled as well by the school as by anyone else.

The experiences of some schools in running voluntary remedial reading classes after school are relevant. At one school where an imaginative and flexible program was launched, the children were given snacks and buttons saying "Reading Club." At another they were given new reading materials. Both of these schools had successful programs. A third school did none of these and used materials from the regular reading class. The program was dropped because the children soon stopped coming.

In other schools, libraries have been opened because of pressure from parents and then are not used by the children. The children are blamed when there are obviously other explanations for the failure of the programs. One immediate question is how complicated is the procedure for using the library? Is it necessary for the child to have a parent come in to sign for him before he can use the library? Is the privilege of taking out books limited to upper-grade children when the need for simple reading materials and stimulation of interest in reading is at least as great in the primary grades?

Schools being used as after-school centers point out the advantage of having the child come after school to a new setting in the same building without getting distracted on the way home. They report no more difficulty in getting the children interested than do centers outside of school. With the large number of children who need help and who respond to offers of help, there will be many available for any program that attempts to be a real service to the children without the rigid atmosphere of a classroom. And there are, of course, children who will not come to any center for help.

In some areas a choice can be made between using schools or outside facilities because both are available. One suburban group developed study centers both in schools and in community buildings. In this instance, the programs conducted in schools have been more successful because they are better. The centers in community buildings have become much more rigid, like another hour of school, whereas those in the schools are more innovative and flexible. There is no guarantee that a project will be good simply because of its location inside or outside of a school building.

A center completely removed from the school has a particular appeal because it is a new setting, away from the one where the child has begun to feel defeated. Such study centers have been organized by local churches and religious groups, settlement houses, boys' clubs, civic associations, PTA's, and housing projects. Study centers can also be completely independent groups. There is no doubt that the same second chance could be given to youngsters within their school buildings, since the rewards of success are genuine wherever they take place.

The minimum staff for an after-school study center, whether in or outside of a school building, is a part-time paid co-ordinator. When there is no paid co-ordinator, members of a volunteer group must accept, on a rotating basis, responsibility for the day-to-day management. In all cases, it is useful to have a citizens' board which meets occasionally to give long-term stability to the effort. A few projects have closed, giving financial reasons for their failure. They were unable to continue as wholly volunteer organizations and could not afford a part-time paid staff position. This paid worker seems crucial to give stability to a project and is usually referred to as the co-ordinator or the site director.

There are no formal requirements for a study center co-ordinator. Human qualities and good sense are most important. The job is usually held by a student or a housewife, but it could as easily be a retired adult. The co-ordinator is not a professional; he or she is a craftsman. The job requires the ability to relate to children, to use volunteers intelligently, and to offer stability to a volunteer program. Some training in education may be helpful for this job.

The salary range depends on local conditions. A salary of $2.00 to $3.00 an hour defines the position. In one suburban area beginning co-ordinators have been hired at $1.25 an hour. Since most of these efforts represent grass roots movements that will have to operate on limited funds, the figure of $2.00 to $3.00 seems most useful for centers in the inner city. In some cases, it may seem more feasible to hire two co-ordinators at $1.50 an hour than to hire a more skilled person for $3.00 an hour. In school systems beginning to experiment with after-school centers, professional teachers have been hired at approximately $6.00 an hour to direct the projects.

There is no typical format for an after-school study center. The following four examples represent a range of different types of centers that operate in a metropolitan community. The first is directed by a YMCA; the second by a boys' club; the third was initiated by a public school and is the only one run on an entirely volunteer basis; and the fourth was created and is directed by a group of interested individuals.

Center 1. This center originated two years ago because of the initiative of a social action committee of a religious group, which maintains a continuing interest in it. The committee handed over direction of the center to a local YMCA, which is now wholly responsible for the project. It provides space and facilities, pays for a part-time co-ordinator, and finances extra needs such as books and supplies. The facilities are multipurpose, being available to the study center group on four afternoons a week from 3:30 to 5:30.

The program is entirely devoted to tutoring; each volunteer has one student at a time, according to a schedule of appointments made out by the co-ordinator, and usually sees two different children in an afternoon. Sixty children are currently being tutored, the majority of them in the nine to twelve age range. Students come for a specific appointment once or twice a week. The library of several hundred donated and purchased books is available only to the sixty children being tutored.

Tutors have been found mainly through word of mouth and are, for the most part, housewives from the neighborhood. The area is middle class and highly residential and is undergoing racial change. Negro children are in the majority at the center. Because students come only by appointment, the atmosphere of this center is close to that of a formal school, but one with a large volunteer staff.

Center 2. This center, associated with a boys' club, is in an all-Negro neighborhood that is very congested and is an area of real cultural deprivation. The center is organized in an informal way.

The center is located in a first-floor, windowless room of a high-rise apartment building. It is a homely, informal, unpretentious room. The club has hired two public school teachers to run the center, assisted by a group of college students from a nearby university. The center provides help with homework, some tutoring, and a friendly home-away-from-home. External activities, ranging from picnics to cultural expeditions, are organized in the summer and continue on some Saturdays throughout the year. About sixty to seventy grade and high school students attend, with or without appointments. Because of the informal atmosphere the center probably does as much for the children in providing them with stimulating and rewarding relationships with adults as it does in helping them to improve their school work.

Center 3. The distinguishing feature of this third center is that it was started by a public school. This public school found that the proportion of its students who were below average in reading ability had in two years increased from 2 to 20 per cent. The school therefore gave its students part-time remedial help after school, and through discussions in the community it prompted a minister and his wife to establish a study center in the basement of a local church.

The center is run by the minister's wife with the assistance of thirty tutors. The majority of the tutors are seniors from the local high school supplemented by other local volunteers, mainly working women. No one is paid for his services.

The program, on Saturday mornings only, is devoted to tutoring in reading and mathematics, and children come only by appointment. The library is stocked by the public library system, since there is no library in the nearby school and the nearest public library is a mile away. The majority of the children are white. Unlike most other local centers, which charge no fee or 25¢ a semester or year, these children pay $1.50 a semester for workbooks and materials.

Center 4. The fourth center was created and is managed by a group of interested residents without benefit of help from any organization. These people have incorporated themselves as a non-profit group and have obtained premises (an old store-front), furnishings, books, and other equipment through their own efforts. They have been helped with generous donations of furniture, books, magazines, and money.

This project was launched in November, 1964, in a deprived and predominately Negro area on Chicago's North Side, but it has already established itself. More than 150 children are registered, most of whom are in need of academic help. At present, children are given tutoring appointments in the evening as fast as volunteers are available, but they can come any time to use the library. There are always some without appointments but they are welcomed. This center is also open in the afternoons for homework help.

There are eighty volunteers, more than half of whom are from the neighborhood. Volunteers ran the center for the first six weeks, but a part-time paid co-ordinator has recently been hired. She is a woman resident of the area with one year of college. Some of the volunteers are employees of business and industrial companies who were urged to participate by their companies. A few have come through church or community organizations. The majority, however, have responded to notices in stores or newspapers or have heard of the project through friends. The volunteers range from high school students to retired adults. The center is a clean, bright spot, very visible and often very audible, in a drab street. It is an autonomous volunteer effort, and it has evoked a dramatic response in an area that has great need of it.

Some social workers and educators have been a source of opposition to volunteer work. Others furnish support for volunteers. Opposition from professional social workers sometimes comes when the volunteers wish to make home or school visits or become more active in the community. When professionals seek to take over the management of study centers, they tend to over-professionalize the staff so that volunteers no longer have the same status, and the program becomes more expensive.

The hours of operation must be set by community needs or the availability of volunteers. Evening programs are often used because the volunteers can come only at that time. In some neighborhoods the streets are full of children in the evening, and an after-supper program is very well attended. In the more middle-class neighborhoods afternoon programs are more frequently used. Often children in such areas would not be allowed to come a distance to an evening program. Saturday programs have been successful, contrary to traditional opinion that children will not come to community activities on this day.

In defining the days for a program to operate, some projects have initially limited themselves to one or two days a week. Since children often seem not to have homework on Friday, this may be a reasonable day for the center to be closed or to offer a special activity such as story-telling, art, or music. The standard operating days have tended to be Monday through

Thursday and Saturday mornings. On school holidays and during the summer vacation, morning hours are usually preferred.

An effective study center relates its efforts to other public and private groups. One group in a deprived area decided to develop a study-recreation program because of the presumed lack of facilities for children in the area. A study of the area revealed under-used recreational facilities and an overwhelming need for academic help. The program was redefined to make the best possible contribution.

A study center is often supportive of other agencies. A common concern is with children who need glasses and whose families are unable to cope with this problem. The cooperation of the study center can be helpful in interpreting known needs of a child to the family and referring the family to other community and welfare agencies.

III

Children in Need of Help

The most impressive aspect in tutoring projects and study centers has been the overwhelming response of children. No one could have predicted that children would respond to these kinds of programs in such large numbers. Throughout the country thousands of children want to come after school for academic help which they know they need. There is no problem of motivation if the proper approach and programs are offered. The efforts of some groups to make these services available to any child who wanted to come have proved impossible. Projects which have not defined a target group have been inundated with children. One project in a deprived area was able to accept only one-sixth of the children who wanted to come. The problem is to sustain interest and involvement by effective academic help.

Since every school in the inner city could use such a facility, it is best for a group to start by working with only one school. The children to be served should be selected in terms of the needs of the school. The principal of the school, because he knows what facilities his children already have, is in a position to help a sponsor define the initial group. In one case, it was third- and fifth-graders who had never or hardly ever managed to complete their homework successfully and who were retarded in reading six months to a year. Encouragement and opportunity to read were their main needs, and this was offered in the form of after-school homework help.

Programs must be adapted to the needs of specific grade levels. Tutoring of preschoolers is inappropriate because volunteers are concerned with academic help. Preschoolers need a good nursery school or kindergarten experience. The facilities of a study center may be used for this age group at other hours and with a program developed especially for them. Often in low-income areas, preschoolers come to a study center with older siblings who are taking care of them. They can be invited to special group activities or included in story time or other ongoing activities of a center. The orientation of a program for these children, however, should come from observation of a good nursery school or day-care center program and not from tutoring projects or study centers.

First- and second-graders do not read well enough to make intensive use of a library setting. They are also often tired at the end of the school day and are not always the best candidates for after-school help. In some communities kindergarteners and first- and second-graders come after supper for individual help. In general, many projects have not had the manpower or facilities to serve this group.

Children in grades three through six respond most willingly to help. Seventh- and eighth-graders do not come so readily when referred by the school or encouraged by parents. It may be their pre-adolescent status, or it may be that their problems are of longer standing. It is striking how much more discouraged they seem to be than the younger children, and their problems seem much harder for volunteers to deal with. The third through the sixth grades, therefore, have become the most frequent group to receive homework and tutoring help after school. In this age group are many children who are six months to two years behind, and the teachers are very often aware of the specific help they need. Children of this age group who are more than two years retarded present greater problems and are not usually candidates for volunteer efforts. There is great need for work with high school students, but these programs are still in the formative stages.

Although a center limits itself to homework help for a specific group, children who do not need this help will ask to come.

These children add a great deal to the atmosphere. If there are library facilities or educational activities that can be made available to all the children, it will help to correct the stigma of the center's being a place for dummies. Children will also hear about a center and come just because they are interested. Sometimes children who do not need help will finish their homework and then help other children. The usual pattern is for a study center to begin with a small number of children referred by the school and then gradually accept others. As children finish tutoring and are able to achieve adequately in school, they may still be left with some need for continued support through group participation.

Another problem in American education is to increase excellence, and some centers have decided to work with an entirely different group for this reason. There are many children doing average work in school who are capable of much more. These children can benefit from the stimulation of a study center. Often they can participate in reading and discussion groups. Establishing such groups as one activity of a center would make it appeal to a more varied group of children. Enrichment and discussion programs often develop as part of a summer program, when trained teachers are available as volunteers. Efforts to help good readers get books from nearby libraries is another aspect of the enrichment program.

RECRUITMENT AND REFERRAL

Many study centers have recruited children by simply opening their doors. Word of mouth, distribution of flyers, and publicity in local community papers brings children. It is imperative to have some kind of school referral form with information on a child so that volunteers are given some simple but meaningful background data. A sample form for both referral and follow-up is included in the Appendix.

Efforts of centers and tutoring programs to recruit their own children have generally worked out well. In one center, thirty children from a public school referred themselves during the first month. When the list was given to the principal, he said that it was an excellent list of candidates. He would have referred most of the same children. Many of them, who were playing in the streets, had already spent hours helping to clean and set up the study center before it opened. They had helped adult volunteers clean the storefront, paint furniture, distribute flyers, and collect and process books. There was a range of ability among these children, however, and the information from the school referral forms indicated how best to help them. Many of them were approximately a year behind in school and were beginning to get discouraged. They were very reachable by volunteer efforts. Some of them were more academically retarded and needed someone with tutoring experience to help them. Some of them did not need remedial work but needed enrichment experiences which could be given in groups. Without the school's active cooperation, the center would not have been able to decide how best to work with them.

Many children will not come simply because the school refers them. Active, personalized efforts to reach these children and their parents may be necessary. Some schools can refer a group of children and have practically all of them show up. From others the children come in much smaller numbers. Since the study center is supposed to be voluntary, it is difficult to know how much persuasion to use. In some cases, word has gotten back to the children who did not come that it is a good place to be, and they come willingly. The school, the parents, and the children all have to understand that this cannot be part of their required school work and that they must come voluntarily. Sometimes children who are getting help or who finish tutoring recruit other children. In one center a boy who graduated from tutoring and remained for homework help brought several shy children by the hand, one at a time, saying, "She wants a teacher."

A tutoring program or study center is not designed to help children with severe emotional problems or those who are mentally retarded. The children accepted for tutoring can and do read. They need encouragement and help to better skills which they already have. Specialized community facilities such as special classrooms and reading clinics are required for more severely handicapped readers.

Study centers should decide just which children they are equipped to serve. The schools can refer children of normal intelligence without severe emotional or physical handicaps who are underachievers. A six-month to two-year retardation is a problem with which supervised volunteers can cope. A non-reader or a child with several years of retardation requires intensive help and more skill than can reasonably be expected of beginning volunteers. Sometimes misguided volunteers want to reach those children who need it most, and they attempt too difficult a task. Building up false hopes in either the children or the staff is unfair.

The schools understand and refer those who are able to use the volunteer help that is available. Teachers have a very good idea which children will be able to relate to a volunteer program. Occasionally, however, if the center is open to all children who want to come, a child will come who has problems of which the staff quickly becomes aware. Such children are usually allowed to use the library and to participate in those activities in which they can, but they are not given individual help unless there is someone of special ability available to work with each of them. As a center is established and becomes well known, some school people or parents will bring in children whom they think need help very much. These may be either retarded children or children with real emotional problems, but no one running a study center needs to feel that the center must be able to help every child whom someone wants to send. There will be times when they will have to say no, and there will be other times when they will let children use part of the facilities without trying to give them individual help that they are not equipped to give.

In any center that operates over a long period, children will come who need special help, and resources may develop to help some of them. For instance, in one center a retarded girl came who was ten years old and could not read. An experienced teacher wanted to help this child and arranged to come several times a week. She was certain that the child could learn to read and was not retarded enough to be institutionalized. The girl did learn to read, and it was a matter of great prestige to her. The girl's poise and determination to be accepted made it possible for her to feel comfortable. In another center, however, a retarded child who was referred had a very difficult time. His referral was a mistake on the part of the school. When the children were tested, he was very embarrassed about putting down his age or any information about himself. He asked the staff person giving the test, "Am I going to get a *U* on this, too?" It seemed a disservice to have this boy in a setting where all he could do was get another *U*. He felt and looked completely out of place. The main difference between these two cases is that there was someone in the first center who was interested in and able to help the girl; for the boy at the second center, this was not true.

THE MEANING OF "DISADVANTAGED"

Children of the inner city are included in a large number who are now called the disadvantaged. These are primarily the children of the poor and include both white and Negro children. Low income by itself does not imply cultural disadvantage, since many poor families do give their children the help and support that they need. Nonetheless, poverty is the chief and common factor in cultural deprivation.

Much has been written about the disadvantaged — their special characteristics, their limited vocabularies, their undeveloped thought processes, and the mental constriction they have suffered because of a lack of preparation for school work. They are truly children of bondage in the sense that their environment is narrow and confining. Nevertheless, it is best to assume that they are more like average children than they are different from them. This is not to hide the differences that do exist, but to emphasize the children's strengths and their potentialities. Like any other group of children, they respond to understanding teachers. They are seeking a sense of dignity and self-identity, and the volunteer who understands them as human beings with potentials for growth will be an effective teacher.

Deprived children often have deprived parents who are unable to give their youngsters some of the basic ingredients required for maturity. In these families, there may not be enough resources to go around, including emotional energy. In the extreme, psychiatrists have found that such parents in crowded living quarters sometimes react to the children as a group instead of as individuals. For instance, if one child annoys them, parents may react by slapping whichever child is nearest. In extreme cases of emotional deprivation, the children fail to develop the minimum self-identity which they must have to cope with their environment.

Learning includes an emotional experience, so ideally a child should come to school with a strong sense of individual worth and self-respect or achieve these feelings early in school. Self-respect is the basic need of all disadvantaged children, even when there is not an extreme lack of self-identity. Kindergarten and first-grade teachers who work successfully wtih such children in our city schools use the children's names extensively as a first means of impressing them with the fact that they are individuals. The teachers use the names of the children in phonics, in songs, and in daily conversation as an effective first step in bringing about self-awareness and self-respect.

Aside from their psychological and social immaturity, these children also lack much of the know-how that would help them succeed in school. Success in school depends upon a whole set of middle-class experiences and values.

Learning involves exploration, and many children have been discouraged from both the physical exploration of their environment and the mental exploration of asking questions, talking, and listening. They have not been listened to or read to as much as other children. Even when the value of education has been impressed upon them, their parents have been less able to prepare them for success in school. Encouragement and opportunities to see and hear are negligible and physical skills with such school materials as scissors and crayons may not be developed as well as it is in other children of the same age. The traditional prereading experiences which are offered in kindergarten may also not be meaningful to these children because of their background.

In deprived areas teachers are aware that many of the materials and methods they use, geared to the middle-class suburban child, are quite foreign to the lives of the children they teach. They sometimes feel that they are teaching English as a "foreign language." They have found that they can assume very little by way of a common experience among disadvantaged city children.

The initial attitude of deprived children toward school can be described as neutral, in contrast to the positive attitude of middle-class children. Middle-class children have been impressed with the value of learning and may have a conception of reward for intellectual effort. Even in the absence of an appropriate background, disadvantaged children still express a basically friendly attitude during the earliest school experiences. For a long time teachers have been impressed with how these essentially curious and receptive children change in attitude later and become hostile or apathetic as they fail in school. Children must learn to read early in school because later school success can now be predicted quite accurately by the end of the third grade.

Some previous ideas about the disadvantaged child have had to be revised. For years people talked about the broken homes of these children as their great disadvantage compared to middle-class children. To come from a broken home is a real disadvantage. But it has recently been found that although the home is broken in the legal sense, lower-class children often do have the support of an extended family that is not available to middle-class children with their small families and high mobility. The broken home is no less a problem, but the positive aspects of lower-class families were not considered before.

The term "culturally deprived" seems especially unfortunate. To speak of children as disadvantaged seems more accurate and appropriate. It makes clear that we are talking about advantages that some children have not had. The danger with any term used to describe the children of the poor is that the differences be tween such children and others come to be more important than the similarities. Some people, impressed with the differences, have decided that a different type of education is the answer. Although better and more imaginative materials are obviously needed in our schools, the right of every child to a basic competence in academic skills should be of more concern than questions of his differences.

The failure rate among disadvantaged children is very high. Some schools in deprived areas have found that as much as 40 per cent of the total failing in the school occurred at the end of the first grade. Eighty-five per cent of the failures occurred before the third grade level. So it is in these early years that children have been labeled failures; and in most cases this failure involved reading since this is the most crucial criterion in deciding who will fail. The children who have been allowed to get by because of the reluctance of schools to fail more children are equally handicapped because they have to struggle to achieve in work that is beyond their development.

From some reports one would gather that disadvantaged children are inarticulate and unimaginative. Since our orientation is that similarities between these children and others are much more important than the differences, we want to know more about their strengths than we do now. The loyalty of these children impresses anyone who has ever helped them. Their ability to help younger children and their sense of responsibility in taking care of younger children seems as great if not superior to that of middle-class children. Their willingness to identify with people who help them and thereby help others has been impressive.

These children are not articulate, and speech is one of their biggest problems. But they talk very freely to each other, and when they tell stories they can be very expressive. They often do not use punctuation or capitalization in their written work and sometimes write stories which they have to read to us. They do not know standard children's games that we teach them. On the other hand, an observer in a large city reported that a group of poor children playing with only a bushel basket with the bottom broken out and a ball made up fifty different games to play with that equipment.

At the centers we have been impressed that as they learn to read better, they also learn to express themselves better. They do have a good feeling for rhythm and enjoy poetry. Often poetry is used by a volunteer with one child alone; other times, group choral reading of poems has met with great success. The children who read poorly seem to enjoy it the most. They follow along carefully reading every word they can and chime in on any chorus. Schools have often recognized the sense of rhythm that these children have by letting them sing. Since poor speech is so common, help in reading should include work in developing better speech. A lot of this may be just not knowing what reading is supposed to sound like. The children are often quite mechanical in their reading, and they often watch an adult as though trying to see what reading is supposed to sound like. We notice then that they read as we do. In one case, a little Negro girl now reads with the New York accent of her volunteer. This does not carry over into her speech, but she has absorbed this as part of what reading is.

The children with whom volunteers work also show a mixture of immaturity and sophistication. There is no doubt that children from poorer families have assumed more responsibility in the home, particularly with their younger siblings. Their premature sophistication is often accompanied by a lack of basic knowledge about the world. It is a maturity that seems to be out of line with many of their abilities, sometimes seeming to be a cover-up for lack of real maturity. Whatever the reason, we assume it is part of the groping for self-respect and self-esteem that all children share. It is possible to appreciate the positive aspects of this maturity and not be overwhelmed with the fact that a child may have been so busy helping at home that she has not been taught what right and left mean or how to tell time.

THE STRUGGLE FOR SELF-ESTEEM

One of the problems of inner city poor children is the residential mobility of their families that continually disrupts their school life. This mobility and its consequences become apparent to volunteers. Children of the inner city have often moved many times during their school lives and more frequently than middle-class children. Research shows that excessive residential mobility hampers school achievement, especially of the more promising student. For example, one ten-year-old girl identified most of the states on a map and told of having lived in many of them. The following story, written by a twelve-year-old seventh-grader, is typical.

Part of My Life

On July 28, 1952, I was born in the town of M———, Louisiana. My parents' names are Myrtle and Cannie. My father died six months after I was born. I am the thirteenth child from the oldest.

When I began in school I was going to Alto School. I went there three years. I transferred to Eula D. Britton when I was in fourth grade.

When I was in fourth grade I went to Texas to visit my sister in the summer with my brother and his family. That was in July. My birthday was the 28th of July. I had a birthday party and I went to Galveston Beach. We came back in September to go to school. Then I was in fifth grade.

When I was promoted to sixth grade that summer, first I went to Mississippi and then I went back to Texas to visit my sister again.

In Mississippi I was there for July 4. I went on a picnic with my family and friends. I stayed in Mississippi for about a month and a half. Then I went back to Texas. In Texas I had fun. I went to movies, parties and the beach. Then I left Texas and came back to Louisiana. I stayed in Louisiana for about two weeks. Then I left and went back to Mississippi to go to school. I went to a school called Kings. I went there for about four months and then came back to Louisiana.

When school was out I came to Chicago with my sister. I came up here in July. In the months before school started we had picnics and went to parks. We also went to the museum.

Now I go to ——— School. I'm in seventh grade now. This is all I had to say about my life. I have enjoyed every bit of my life.

A fifth-grader joined a new study center and attended twice a week for four weeks, until the family moved again. He was obviously a bright child. His tutor wondered why he didn't know his multiplication tables. He never asked for help, but when it was offered to him he soaked up all he could get. One time he spent one-and-a-half hours doing seven long-division problems. He tried to divide six into a figure and thought seven might work. He therefore wrote down seven sixes and added them up — 12 and 12 and 12 and 6. When that did not work, he tried another number. The staff was impressed with his powers of concentration and his eagerness for help. A volunteer offered to give him one multiplication table to take home and asked if perhaps there was someone at home who would check it. He said that his father would. By the next day, he had learned one table quite well and wanted another. In this manner he learned most of his multiplication tables. During the third week he told the staff that he was moving out of the state the following week. Even in four weeks he received real help with his academic work because of his native intelligence and his desire to learn. Now he will have to make a new adjustment to a new school.

In another center, a ten-year-old boy from a poor family came for reading help. A simple test showed that he was two years behind in reading. He said during the testing that he wanted to be a doctor and impressed the volunteer with his very good basic intelligence and with his pronounced lack of general knowledge. For his first leasson the volunteer brought a book on human physiology along with reading materials, and this book especially fascinated the boy. He had lots of questions and repeated his interest in studying medicine. When the boy did not return the following week, the volunteer phoned his home and received no answer. The father's number was listed separately (he did not live with the family), and the volunteer called him and found that the boy and his mother had suddenly moved to another section of the city. The father said that the boy had not known about the move — "They just decided suddenly one night to move." The tutor told the father that she was very sorry because the boy had seemed so eager to have help with his reading and was obviously a very capable boy. The tutor said that it would be most helpful if the boy could remain in one school, since he would always have a hard time getting caught up in school if he continually moved. The father seemed genuinely interested and wanted to know, "Do you really think it is so important?" She said that she did, and the father seemed appreciative about her concern. They discussed the possibility of the child's coming back for weekly lessons, but it seemed impractical and they both agreed that the family should seek help for the child in their new neighborhood.

Another first-grader who never missed a day at a study center came in one day looking very unhappy and confided to the co-ordinator that he was moving "tonight." He had just been told of the move and did not know where the family was moving. Since he lived close to the center, he was sent home to get the new address. Some of the staff members assured him that they would give the address to his regular volunteer who was not there that day so that she could send him a card. He went out-doors and picked dandelions and handed one to each of the regular staff members without a word. He stayed until closing time, looking as though he had lost his last friend. A walk and an ice cream cone with a staff member helped a little. His deep unhappiness and the few hours that he was allowed to prepare himself for this sudden move left a deep impression on the staff. Work with children like these makes the staff of an after-school center appreciative of the task of inner city teachers and of the difficulties the children face.

The problem of mobility cannot be used as an excuse for fail-ing to work with these children. Possibly, there will be oppor-tunities for referring the children to a new center in their new neighborhood. There are also children who travel long distances or whose parents travel long distances to bring them back to the center. Schools and after-school centers can make a positive con-tribution to family stability by becoming a reason for parents to want to stay in a neighborhood for the benefit of their children. There is evidence that parents who had planned to move de-cided not to because their children gained so much from belong-ing to a special school program or an after-school center. Much of the residential mobility is a reaction to frustration and is with-out design or purpose except for a vague hope of a new chance.

Children who cannot achieve adequately often compensate by exaggerating the extent of their abilities. There is often real confusion about what they can do. Their reports about their school work are often inaccurate. The children will claim that they got only a few answers wrong, but when volunteers go over the paper with them, they find a great many mistakes. There is always something positive that can be said about their work, but it is important that the children be helped to realize their limitations.

In the same way, children will often say, "I want to be a doctor," or "I want to go to college." Many volunteers will say that this is fine without feeling any obligation to explain what these ambitions imply. Often the child who makes such statements is one who is very far behind academically, never does his homework, and has exaggerated ideas of his own ability. One of the challenges in training volunteers is to help them handle such affairs realistically without shattering the children's hopes.

Studies have been done showing that non-achieving children of sixteen to seventeen still express ambitions of wanting to be doctors, lawyers, and engineers. Such findings have been used to argue that they have the same aspirations that so-called middle-class children have. Actually, it proves nothing of the kind. It only proves that these children are guilty of very wishful thinking. Some of this shows up in the very early grades, and sometimes the best help that can be given to a child is to point out the reality of his actual performance.

The lack of knowledge and the confusion they have about the world sometimes extends to themselves. Children of the inner city often express confusion about their ages. Many of them do not know when their birthdays are or how old they are. Part of this is reluctance to admit that they are older than they should be for their grade level because they have failed in school. Aside from these youngsters, however, there are many others who are genuinely confused about their birthdays and ages. They sometimes believe they are older or younger than their mothers say they are.

We claim to have abandoned the philosophy in teaching that "the child is an empty vessel for us to fill." But because of the pressure of school and because of concern with how much these children do not know, they are often not given an opportunity to give anything. One child wrote about a volunteer, "I like Jean because she lets me help her." These children, more than most children, want the chance to give something. The first evidence of this need is in their desire to show anyone what they can do. Often an interested adult has a great deal of success just by being interested and listening and watching. One little boy who was offered reading help by an adult was told, "I would like to help you with your reading because I'm good at that, but don't ask me to help with arithmetic because I'm not very good at that." The little boy's eyes got very big and he looked up at her and said, "I'll help you with arithmetic because I'm good at that." She told him that would be fine, and at the end of each reading lesson he showed her some of the arithmetic he knew. She did not spoil it by claiming that he taught her the arithmetic or by telling him that this was really so simple that she already knew it. Instead, she accepted his need to give as a valid need and let him show her what he could do at the end of each lesson for several weeks.

Parents, too, have brought gifts of fruit to staff people. A mother offered to bake cookies for a center because she felt that she could not help in the academic program, and she wanted to contribute. Another offered to make curtains. One mother brought her small child for a lesson every Saturday morning and liked to read to a group of younger children. Another liked to play games with a group of children while her own son had his reading lesson. It was a matter of great prestige to her that she was able to help. It is important that the need to give be recognized and accepted.

In reporting to parents, volunteers try to behave as any good teacher would. There is always something positive to be said about any child's behavior or progress. Appreciation of this and of the parents' efforts in seeing that the child does come to do his work are valued by the parents. Often there is some suggestion of what the parents can do that will help the school and the center. Usually, it is the suggestion that someone at home listen to the child read a few minutes each evening or go over some work with him. Again, this is offering the parents a chance to give something.

Tutoring projects and after-school study centers are primarily concerned with children who need help in school. In working toward this goal, it is necessary to involve the parents wherever possible and to get their active support. But volunteer workers are clearly best able to help the youngsters. It is sometimes argued that effective educational programs would strain the relations of children with their parents in the inner city. Morally or socially there is no basis for this view. It is true that a deprived parent may be resentful of the progress of his children, and therefore it is important to help him help his child by encouraging him or at least not interfering. But education has been and is now more than ever the central institution for improving one's lot and one's personal competence. To deny the existence of these desires in the deprived family is both an error and a subtle form of snobbery.

IV

Program and Activities

Within the four walls of a study center, a wide variety of programs and activities can go on at the same time. In fact, the strength of the study center or tutoring project is its flexibility and multiple purpose; thus a casual visitor may be startled by what appears to be a lack of order and routine. What he is observing are efforts at supplementary academic help in the form of homework help or tutoring, group activities involving writing and speech, educational games, and rewarding leisure-time activities.

HOMEWORK HELP

It's fun to do homework at McKinley — it ain't fun at home.
REMARK OF A NINE-YEAR-OLD BOY

Homework is usually the immediate school task that children face, and their ability to complete it successfully means immediate reward the next day in school. It shows volunteers what is expected of the child. Helping him do the job reveals his abilities to function at his present grade level.

Volunteers do not do homework for children, although they try to be as helpful as necessary. Sometimes, at first, it seems that they do everything except the writing. The aim is always to help the child help himself, but since these children have poor work habits, it takes time to teach them to be able to work alone.

Some children only need the assurance of helpful adults. They often want to show adults what they have to do and then may sit waiting until someone suggests how to begin. They often have to have words of assurance, "I'm here to help you if you need it."

If children have the same homework assignment, an adult can help five or more at the same time. Five is a maximum group when the children have never or have hardly ever finished their work successfully. In the beginning they need a great deal of personal support even with assignments that they understand. The advantage is that some explanation and help can be given to a group.

Homework help is easier to organize than individual tutoring as a new program develops in the inner city. Three adults can help a group of about fifteen children. The immediate response and praise from the teachers helps to keep enthusiasm going after the first week or two. The children also support each other. After the honeymoon period of about three weeks in one project, some of the children began to suggest skipping the homework and having other activities first. A couple of children always objected, "Let's get it done so they can check it."

A standard complaint from the children is, "The teacher didn't explain it." Study center staffs assume, as parents do, that the teacher did explain the work. They also assume that the children may not understand the work even after an explanation. Sometimes another child will say, "Sure she did — you just didn't listen."

Volunteers are not expected to have a special background in school subjects except possibly in mathematics. They are expected to be able to help a child read his assignment and to encourage him to do it as the teacher requests. By using the children's textbooks, volunteers can see how the work was presented. It is also often good to encourage the child to ask for more help at school. He can go to the teacher after class and ask for help if he is reluctant to ask during class. It is good for children to know that adults do not have all the answers.

Volunteers are often concerned about mathematics. Most of the mathematics that puzzle study center children involves the processes of addition, subtraction, multiplication, and division. They are often limited by not knowing such facts as the multiplication tables or by not understanding which process to use to solve a problem. Some adults are better equipped to explain this than others, but volunteers should not assume that they are not equipped to help. They can always offer some help and can study the child's textbook with him.

The behavior of one worker is typical of the inadequate feelings volunteers often express. A volunteer came excitedly to another staff member and said, "This boy has seventh-grade arithmetic, and I'm sure I can't help him." The regular staff member suggested they look at the assignment. It was subtraction of four-place numbers. Asked if he knew how to do it, the boy said yes. Asked if he knew how to prove the answers, he showed that he did. He was typical of the children who ask for help and really need only an assurance of interest from the adult.

In another homework center, the children were working with fractions. The staff had not studied these for a long time. One staff member studied the textbook and interpreted to the other staff members as they helped the children. The assignment was long, and everyone worked very hard. It was important to the children to see that adults also have to understand instructions and follow them. It was especially impressive to the children that volunteers were willing to work so hard to help them.

Homework is often difficult because the child's abilities are not up to his grade level. At the same time, it can be very important for him to return to school with a completed paper or with one that shows reasonable effort. Therefore, volunteers usually concentrate first on the task at hand. They may say, "I know this is hard, but do what you can and I will help you." Often volunteers are successful in giving background help along with the current assignment. A child may be doing compass work, and a volunteer realizes that he does not know his directions. In teaching these the volunteer discovers that the child does not know left from right. The volunteer is able to give help in a way that is both remedial and meaningful for tomorrow's lesson.

A volunteer is often able to see some of a child's difficulties that a classroom teacher misses. One child failed a test in addition. Her homework assignment was to do it over. In doing addition she added correctly, but with a first-column sum of 12 she would write down the 1 and carry the 2. This was a consistent error throughout the test.

Successful homework help will lead to the child's being able to assume responsibility for his own work. Volunteers see this develop and encourage it. One girl finished all except two of her arithmetic problems at a center. It was closing time, and the co-ordinator suggested that she finish at home now that she understood how to do them. The girl looked unsure and concerned as she left. The next day she came immediately to the co-ordinator and said, "I did the last two myself and they were right!"

INDIVIDUAL TUTORING

When a child is assigned for tutoring, the volunteer should be given at least a reading score, the child's grade level and birth date, and the name of his teacher. The reading score may be several months old, but it gives some indication of his reading level. If the score is 3.2, it means that his reading ability is at the level of the second month of third grade. A score of 3.5 means middle third-grade level. Since the score represents an average of different kinds of reading ability, the child's actual ability in one area such as vocabulary or comprehension may be below the average.

By knowing a child's grade in school, a volunteer avoids the possibility of embarrassing him. The children are also often vague about the names of their teachers, and this can be embarrassing to them. In some tutoring projects, the students are called "tutees" by the staff. Such labeling seems pointless and may in fact be an expression of condescension.

When meeting a child for the first time, a volunteer should be sure to know his name and pronounce it properly or ask him. We also want the children to know volunteers as individuals. Therefore, the volunteer should tell the child his name, write it for him, and should tell the child what he wishes to be called. The volunteer ought to give the child a little information about himself, where he grew up, where he lives, and especially exactly when he will be available to see the student. Each child should have a folder, which can be a large manilla envelope, to carry his materials home in. The name of the tutor and the appointment times should be printed on a card and put into this folder. Some volunteers repeat this for several lessons, if the child loses the card, until they feel that it is unnecessary. Some give the children their telephone numbers so that the child can call if he will have to miss a lesson.

Many volunteers are frankly fearful of the first meeting. It helps them to know that the children are usually as fearful as they are. For many children it is the first experience at being alone with an adult other than their parents.

Some projects have an inventory of questions for children to fill out or for volunteers to ask a child. These immediately seem to place a barrier between the child and the volunteer. The introduction should be brief, and the best approach is to offer some reading materials as soon as possible.

Unfortunately, in some projects volunteers have probed prematurely into the backgrounds of their pupils. One project actually used a form which asked children if they were white, Negro, or other; if their mothers were on ADC; and facts about the education of their parents. Another group designed a form that asked children how they got along with siblings and whether their friends were usually the same age, older, or younger. Such information cannot be worth the discomfort it may cause. An important contribution of a volunteer is respect for a child's privacy. This does not mean that he does not dare to show interest in a child, but that he is sensitive to the responses. A casual question such as, "Have you always lived in Chicago?" will show interest.

Since the children come for specific reading or arithmetic help, the tutor should have materials ready. If the child brings his work, it is easier to start with that. The children know that they are there for help, and it often seems best to relieve uncertainty by getting right to work. The teacher may have made specific suggestions which can be explained. By knowing the reading level, the tutor can have a couple of books ready. (In the absence of a test score, the simplest quick check of reading is to have excerpts from graded readers typed on white cards. When a child makes only two or three errors a page, it is a satisfactory level to work in. There is an abundance of material available in public libraries marked by grade level.)

If the beginning reading is easy for the child, he has a sense of achievement and can go on to the next level. If he has to go back to simpler material because a tutor overestimated his ability, it is another defeat for him. Success is especially important for these children since they have had so little of it, and that is another reason for making the first reading easy.

We do not want children to get the idea that they are referred for outside help because they are the hopeless or worst readers. This is by no means true, since we deliberately plan to help mainly where there is strong evidence that the child can do better. It may help to say that many children of various ages and ability have come for help. The reading score will show something about the extent of help needed. One time to offer reassurance would be after the child successfully reads easy material. Then a tutor can honestly say that he reads well at that level but that schoolwork at his present level must be difficult. Tutoring will offer him a chance to catch up on some reading skills so that schoolwork will be more rewarding to him. The words fun and easy are overworked in children's publishing. Since reading is neither fun nor easy for these children, an appeal to maturity and academic success is a more honest approach.

Volunteers have an enormous advantage to support and help a child without the pressure of a fixed curriculum. They do not have to teach any specific skill in any specific way. They do have a responsibility, however, to support the child's need to achieve academically and to gain in self-respect. Volunteers are not expected to be either reading teachers or remedial reading experts. It helps them, nevertheless, to know something about teaching in general and the problems of learning to read.

The basic principles of teaching reading have not changed very much in recent years. What has changed is the wealth of materials that may cause a beginning tutor to wonder where to begin. A first grade reader published in 1900 mentions "phonics, the need for familiar material, and the repetition of words for reinforcement." Fortunately, the old controversy between sight reading and phonics training is no longer important. It is now commonly believed that reading is a complicated process involving both kinds of skills. Children start with sight words in first grade, but they already have had some prereading work in kindergarten, and phonics work is continued through the early years of reading.

Most reading is taught by the use of one of the standard readers. These are meant to teach the mechanics of how to read and only the mechanics. The task of the teacher is easier if the child has been read to and is motivated to read because of the image of older people who do read. Even then, the readers have to be interpreted because the few words used tell only part of a story. "Look, look" requires a knowledge of who is speaking, to whom, and about what. Whole words are introduced slowly and repeated often. In a normal classroom, ability ranges from those who may learn new words with one presentation to those who learn very slowly. Reading groups are usually assigned so that children can work and progress at their ability level.

There are supplementary books at every reading level that use the same words in different ways to give helpful reinforcement. Poor readers often do not supplement the reader with other books and may not read outside of school, so even over a summer vacation they lose some ability and need review.

The principles of tutoring are the same as those of any other teaching. We try to start from where the child is (not in grade placement but in actual achievement) and to motivate him to continue by offering teaching in logical, sequential steps to the next level. He learns by having what is taught related to what he already knows and reinforced by using the same words in different contexts, and by feelings of reward for his efforts. Sometimes it is a matter of bringing some reading skills up to the level of the others. Often the classroom teacher has a very clear idea of the child's troubles and can help with suggestions. We have found that by observation and the use of corrective teaching materials we can find some of the problems that cause a child to fail in reading, and we can help him to read better. Even a little help often gives him such a boost that he is more willing to try. Parents and teachers have been able to see the success that, in turn, encourages him to go further.

Reading problems are of many types, but there are some general patterns. Many children do not know enough about phonics, although they all have had some in school. They are unable to sound out words, so they either falter or substitute something vaguely similar to what is in the book. They often know the sight vocabulary and little else. A volunteer can demonstrate how to approach a new word by beginning with the initial sound, covering up part of the word, and pronouncing the syllables to see if the child can figure it out. It is better not to discuss root words unless the tutor is sure of himself. One volunteer helped a child with root words and pointed to "on" as a root for "only." The two words are completely unrelated, and such misinformation only confuses the child. Phonics books help to review the sounds of letters. They are also used to review particular combinations of letters that seem troublesome.

Other children know how to sound out big words, but miss the small ones or confuse them constantly. All second- and third-graders confuse some of these words. If there is a pattern of continual confusion, a basic word set can be used to see just how many of these sight words are a problem. (These sets of two hundred words make up 75 per cent of the material in primary readers.) They are sometimes called "popper" words because they have to be memorized, like the multiplication tables, so that they can be immediately recognized. These words, such as when, where, then, and there, can be presented in small groups to be studied and memorized. A simple test form sometimes used consists of a check list of the words to be checked off as they are shown to the child. Or, a few can be used at a time and the ones the child misses kept separately for him to work with. The volunteer can explain their meanings and use them in sentences.

Besides visual and phonetic clues, reading also depends on contextual clues. If a child reads the sentence, "The dog lapped up the milk with his little red _____," and hesitates, it is better to ask what makes sense. These children often have to be encouraged to make reasonable guesses. Comprehension exercises are available that ask questions to test general and specific comprehension. Sometimes the subject matter of the workbooks and exercises for comprehension seems unappealing. Library books may interest a child more and lead to better discussion. Volunteers do have to discuss some materials with the child to see that he does understand what he reads.

Volunteers are often impressed with how mechanical reading is for children who are retarded in reading. The words in the books seem to have no meaning; they certainly are not understood as communication. Older children in one group were assigned parts in a simple story and were startled to find that the phrases in quotation marks represented what the characters said. The phrase "said John" had meant nothing to them until they were assigned parts of the story to read aloud.

Even with appealing material that the children choose and seem to enjoy, they may seem at a loss to discuss what they have read. It often helps to personalize the reading by asking, "How would you feel if your team lost the big game of the season as the Hornets did?" One child reported that he had read a cool book, *The Cat in the Hat*. Asked what it was about, he said, "A cat." He was unable to tell any more about the story until he was asked, "How would you feel if someone did that to your mother's best dress?" He began to talk about his reactions to the story and was able to remember the events in sequence. From his first reaction, an inexperienced volunteer might have concluded that the child knew nothing about the story.

Children who enjoy reading identify with many characters and situations. It is the volunteer's task to find material that will appeal to children who have not developed this ability. A volunteer read a deep-sea adventure with a child. At the end of a chapter, in an exciting part of the story, the child suddenly said, "Let's quit." The volunteer said, "But the diver is under water with his air hose broken. Don't you want to see how he gets out?" The boy said, "Why? T'aint me." Asked if he would like to write a story, the child was immediately interested.

Children in schools and study centers write or dictate some of their own materials. One school has experimented with duplicating stories written by fifth-graders and giving them to primary children to read. They often consider them superior to their readers. Older boys are often able to dictate or write stories about baseball or football using words they would not be able to read in a textbook. They are usually able to read what they have written or dictated after it is typed.

In both reading and writing, the children translate words into their own grammar. If the result still makes sense, volunteers try not to discourage them by continually interrupting. At the end of a unit or a story, part of the discussion can include new words or expressions for the ones the child used.

In dictating stories, children also use their own grammar. One child dictated, "For supper I et . . ." and the volunteer wrote down "ate." The child told her it was wrong and she said, "That is how the word is spelled." He was very insistent that she had the wrong word. In general, if a word or phrase becomes an issue, it is better for the adult to give in and assure a child that he can use any word he chooses in his stories. In this case, the volunteer was simply wrong as far as the child was concerned. "Et" is a standard word in rural areas. Even if other children later criticize him, he may accept correction from them more easily than from adults.

Good readers develop different kinds of reading skills, depending on their use of reading. A novel or a daily paper does not require the same degree of concentration as a professional paper. Children can be helped to use their reading in different ways. Sometimes they enjoy bringing a news article which they are able to understand. For study purposes they need to learn to get both general information and specific details when these are considered important. The advantage of some workbook materials is that they teach specific study skills such as understanding the main thought of a paragraph, outlining ideas in sequence, or identifying specific answers.

At first, a volunteer has to explain and discuss material without always knowing how clearly the child does understand. When the children feel comfortable they begin to ask for explanations. One ten-year-old boy wanted to know what a "world's record" meant. He knew about phonograph records, but that did not make sense. A volunteer explained that many English words have several meanings and asked if he could think of any other way he had heard the word record used. He thought a moment and said, "Yeah — a police record." He was pleased that he had remembered another meaning by himself; then the volunteer explained world record.

Tutors watch for any sign of interest as a starting point. They sometimes ask the child what he is interested in, realizing that if these children had well-defined interests, some kind teacher or librarian would have helped them find appropriate materials. If there is an expressed interest in anything, it gives a tutor somewhere to begin to look for books. If the child prefers baseball, the tutor wants to know because he can find books about baseball and baseball heroes. At the same time, he offers a variety of books and encourages variety in reading because his big task is to develop interests. Since many of the children are non-verbal, it is hard to discover their interests. From one lesson to the next, the tutors watch for response to whatever they offer and consult with each other for help.

Many children enjoy being read to. Others seem overwhelmed by the closeness or the superior reading ability of the tutor. At first, the reading may be limited to introducing the books the child may read at home. Volunteers sometimes listen to a child read the first several pages, or they look through the book with him for unusual words. As a minimum introduction, the names of the characters in the story ought to be introduced. The tutor encourages the children to ask for help at home with words they do not know. Some of the children's parents are known to be illiterate, but several children have an older brother or sister who can help them.

If a child is referred for help in arithmetic, a score should again be included in the referral. Many of the children who need reading help also need help in arithmetic, particularly when they begin to get word problems which they cannot read. Since the new math involves more reading earlier, there may be more concern with arithmetic. The use of the child's textbook, of course, is the easiest way to know how to help him. Often, however, the teacher will make specific suggestions about what a child needs in arithmetic. In the absence of help from the school or from the textbook, it is still possible to identify some of a child's difficulties by making up problems for him. It is also possible to take an imaginary trip, by saying something like, "Pretend that you are 21 and have your driver's license and a car. You and a friend have jobs in Cleveland, and you are going there to work. Let's pretend that you each have a certain amount of money for the trip and you are going to share expenses." Perhaps a map is available to make it possible to estimate how long the trip will take and when they should start in the morning. The cost of gas for the trip can be figured out and deducted from the expense account. This can be continued throughout the trip, planning expenses and deducting them. By the time an imaginary trip is finished, a tutor has some idea of the child's ability to handle arithmetic facts. The same work can be done as a review, and combinations that trouble the child may be written on cards to study.

The children often count on their fingers. Efforts of volunteers to distract them sometimes lead to subterfuge — like that of the child who clicked her tongue against her teeth to hide the fact that she needed to count. Most children like to manipulate such objects as toothpicks, buttons, or counters. Sheets of paper showing such basic mathematical facts as sums that add up to 5 or 6, or all the multiplication tables are good references. The numbers from 1 to 10 are written across the page horizontally and down the page vertically. The tables are filled in by multiplying each horizontal number across the page with each vertical number. Problems that are made up by a volunteer may appeal to a child more than those from a book, or the child may try to make up some for the adult. An adult should never pretend to miss problems or not to know the answers, thinking that it will make a child more comfortable. But an adult can tell a child that he is going to make mistakes and wants the child to catch him and explain why he is wrong.

Although a tutor's attitude should always remain positive and encouraging, experience shows that the children's need for continual help and approval gradually lessens as they gain in skill. A common thread running through the reports of tutors is the continual need for support and encouragement at first, and a gradually growing willingness and ability to work alone. Everyone responds better to praise and assurance of success, but only honest praise is meaningful to children. They are much more honest than adults and respond more to the attitudes of people than to their words. If an adult's basic attitude is, "This kid is surely never going anywhere," the child is apt to sense it, no matter what words the adult uses.

These children are apt to tire easily because they have already had a day in school. In addition, children who do not learn to read often have used a great deal of energy to keep from learning. Although they want very much to be helped, they have to overcome years of habits of not learning and not achieving. The lesson should therefore be flexible. Some children become fascinated with the reading or phonics materials and want to continue for a half hour. Others become tired, and it makes more sense to allow the child to relax, to listen to a story, or to have a few minutes of fun.

Many tutors offer a small reward for every five or ten books reported on. A notebook is made up of theme paper, with a construction-paper cover, for the child to carry home in his folder. Original stories can be encouraged, and should count as book reports. Sometimes the children give the reports orally at first, but a tutor can learn more about their reactions to books and what materials to offer later by having even a one-sentence report about the books. Encourage the child to tell whether he liked the book and why. The very idea that books can be criticized is new to some children. The fact that someone is concerned with his interests and wants to know what he would like to read may be important to him.

The tutoring sessions normally last anywhere from 30 minutes to an hour. Each session should be regularly scheduled for a set period of time. One session a week is the minimum. Generally, two lessons a week are preferred and are assumed to be much more helpful. Thirty minutes, twice a week, may be all that the tutor can give. Sometimes the lessons are set for 45 minutes. Some children hate to let go and stay an hour and then leave reluctantly. If the session is limited to once a week, 45 minutes or an hour ought to be possible. But if a tutor feels that a child is uncomfortable and it would help to end early, he should. Whatever the volunteer has decided as the time he can spend should be the limit, and he may have to say, "That's enough work for today," or "Our time is up for today."

Volunteers are often unduly concerned with making mistakes. Since tutoring is a learning situation, they will make mistakes just as parents and teachers do every day. Children are amazingly flexible and responsive. They may respond with facial expressions instead of words, but their reactions tell the most about the success or failure of the lesson.

Volunteers must structure a lesson and yet give a student reasonable opportunities for making choices. A volunteer who says "what do you want to do?" is not behaving as a responsible tutor. Remember the experience of the teacher who asked a child in a reading group, "Do you want to read the next page?" The child smiled and said no. The teacher turned to another child and said, "Read the next page," and tried in the future not to offer children choices that were not really valid. The limit of choices also makes them comprehensible. To offer books in a library where there are hundreds of choices is not as good as to offer two or three selections that the tutor can introduce by discussing the subject matter, the characters, and the plots.

There should be in every lesson some element of success. Volunteers are trying to reverse the continual pattern of failure children have known by experiences of success. This success may be in demonstrating skill in arithmetic, if the child is more competent in that subject, or in drawing. After a lesson a volunteer can ask himself, "What success did this child have today?"

Even the way criticism is given is important. One tutor asked, "Do you know that a period means a stop?" Obviously the child had to say yes or appear stupid. It would be better to say matter-of-factly, "A period means the end of a sentence. See if you can show me where the sentences end by pausing there." Then praise the child's efforts.

A volunteer is not a classroom teacher and has a dual responsibility to give meaningful help and simultaneously show the child that reading can be a rewarding or purposeful activity. Since they do not have a captive audience, volunteers have found it better not to assign definite homework. It is fine to suggest material to the child and send it home with him. If a volunteer assigns work, the child is in difficulty if he does not do it. He may either stay away from the next lesson or become belligerent or unhappy because he has again failed. By not imposing assignments, the volunteer can continue with the work in the next lesson and wait for the relationship to become meaningful enough that the child wants to help himself.

The most important asset a volunteer can have is an attitude of giving freely. Especially with children who feel that they have failed or that society has failed them, an attitude of respect and willingness to give freely with no strings attached is most important. This assumes that the volunteer will have materials ready. Many volunteers have their own folders with such supplies as books to read with or to a child, a magic slate, and crayons or colored pencils. The children may ask for these supplies, and the tutor can assure them that they will be available next week.

Some volunteers become concerned with the children's requests and ought to understand that much of this is normal testing. It is fine to give the children presents for birthdays and special events. Spontaneous gifts can often be even more rewarding, but they should be the decision of the adult so that they do not interefere in the relationship. Such gifts need not be elaborate. Paperback books or a subscription to the summer edition of *Weekly Reader* that costs 50 cents have been successful gifts. The relationship the adult is offering is the most important gift, and giving refers to an attitude more than to material objects. The difference can be explained with two examples. One child conned an adult into giving him lunch money and then felt so guilty that he did not return to the center for weeks. Another youngster shopped for a simple dictionary with his tutor. The child waxed the cover of the book to protect it and proudly showed it, asking everyone to handle it carefully because "It's my own new book."

Teaching can allow for a great deal of innovation on the part of the teacher. Teachers learn to plan lessons and select materials for their children, but the good ones watch the reactions of their students. They decide when a change of pace is required, and they vary the day's routine when necessary. A tutor does the same, and often tries to have the most difficult part of the lesson early so that the student understands that other activities will follow. Setting time limits also helps. "We will spend ten minutes on this" shows the child that there is a reasonable time limit.

An experienced teacher has developed her own techniques, some of which she will frankly admit are gimmicks. She may send a restless child to get a drink at the drinking fountain farthest from the classroom, knowing that when he returns he will be ready to settle down. She may become tired of saying no and try suggesting something the child can do instead of what he asked to do. Volunteers in the new role of tutor are understandably looking for a method or a gimmick that always works, but there are none. Anyone responsible for their training should be willing to offer materials and suggestions and to give assurance that the volunteer should use only those with which he feels comfortable.

The materials and suggestions are only the first responsibility of the supervising staff. Far more important is the day-to-day help that volunteers need. Suggestions are going to be used and accepted literally without a sense of proportion unless someone helps the volunteers. An example is the suggestion to a group of tutors that children like such word games as rhyming and giving antonyms and synonyms. The volunteers began to watch for words to rhyme or discuss in the children's reading. They continually interrupted the reading, using a valid technique but in a way that destroyed the sense of the lesson. They were, in fact, telling the children that this reading makes so little sense that it is possible to stop or start anywhere. The specific examples given in this chapter are all only suggestions for a volunteer to use in a way that makes sense both to himself and to the individual child.

Sometimes questions arise of how long to keep a child in a tutoring program. Volunteers try to help a child until he is working comfortably at his grade level. This may leave him still in need of homework help so that he will have continued support.

Children sometimes do not like to be dropped from tutoring, and the volunteers often do not want to stop seeing them. There is no reason to discontinue tutoring after a year even if the child is working at his level, but at some point it may seem better for him to transfer to an enrichment group or other group activity.

GROUP ACTIVITIES

Study centers often provide an opportunity for group work with children. Depending upon the available space and program, there will be various opportunities for volunteers to use group games and activities. The children may have returned their library books, finished their homework, or had an individual lesson. They may also be part of a reading and discussion group.

Since these children need help with speech, reasoning, and personal achievement, volunteers in study centers must use a variety of approaches. There are many educational games available at toy stores and school supply stores. These include a wide range of reading and arithmetic activities. Some volunteers also develop original materials.

Speech Activities.— A get-acquainted game such as the following will help the children and staff learn each other's names. Everyone is seated in a circle, and the leader explains that each person will say his name and something that he likes that begins with the same letter, and will try to repeat those names which came before his. She begins by saying, "My name is *C*arol and I like *c*ats." The next player says, "Her name is *C*arol and she likes *c*ats. My name is *D*onald and I like *d*iscs." This continues, with each child repeating who everyone is in order around the circle, and adding his name at the end. Some children cannot remember all the names and items; name tags may help. There are other versions of the same basic game. The leader can say, "I am going on a trip around the world. In my trunk I'm packing an *a*pple." The children take turns repeating this statement and adding items beginning with other letters of the alphabet. Another simple group game consists of having each child make one statement about what he did yesterday or on an imaginary day. One child may then try to reconstruct the day — or the group may do this together.

The children may tell a story cooperatively. The leader begins and then lets the children take short turns in continuing. The leader may have to take other turns to keep the story going. Poetry, short stories, and tall tales are usually good beginning selections for reading to children. Volunteers have used puppets, since the children may talk more easily with such props. They can take turns being performers and audience. They also like to read parts of a play or story.

A helpful introduction to dramatics is the use of skits, which are available at school supply stores. These consist of stories that an adult reads, in which the children supply sound effects at the proper time. In a small group each child is assigned a character; in a larger group several children take a part together. The stories are usually nonsensical, and the children enjoy the active participation they require. Some children, however, find it easier to perform simple charades before any speech activities are attempted.

Such voice chorus activities as reading poetry in unison are enjoyed. Public libraries often have files of poetry that has been used successfully in group speech activities. The children are often inhibited in speech, so at first volunteers offer materials and literally put words in the children's mouths. Later, as the children's abilities develop, such activities could become truly creative by helping the children write and produce their own material.

Children like to record their voices on a tape recorder and listen to themselves. A variety of phonograph records can also be used to advantage. One of the most popular is the sing-along type with accompanying word-sheets.

Writing Activities. — Writing is another good group activity. Inexpensive notebooks or those made from writing paper stapled into a construction paper cover can be given to the children. They can put their names on them or decorate them. Inform the children that when the books are finished, they can take them home.

It may be necessary to give suggestions to start writing. As with individual children, volunteers would not suggest that the children write about home. At first, the study center may be a better topic. The children can write about why they like the center, or how it could be made better. Many of them have pets, favorite holidays, a prettiest dress to describe (real or fantasied), hopes of what they want to do when they grow up, or thoughts about what kind of person each wants to be. Another favorite writing game is to see how many little words can be made from the letters of phrases such as "Abraham Lincoln of Illinois" or "St. Patrick's Day in March." A leader has to know his children and be willing to give suggestions. If the children can be told that some of their writing will be put on the bulletin board and can be assured that drawings and illustrations are equally welcome, they will want to write. At first, it would be best to accept their work without criticism and to mention the strong points instead of showing concern with spelling or grammar. Later, it is important that they receive help and constructive suggestions.

The co-ordinator of one center encouraged the children to write thank-you notes for donations of books and money. Children often have written letters with their tutors' help and enjoyed mailing them. In one case, they seemed surprised when it was suggested that the letters should be mailed. They said that they had no envelopes or stamps, and some had never sent a letter. Envelopes and stamps were provided and the children taken for a walk so they could mail their own letters. Another group of children wrote letters to President Lyndon Johnson, and all received an answer.

Simple printing sets or typewriters may encourage the children to compose stories. Typewriters are prized possessions in some centers, and children sign up for their use. At first, the children seem to type letters indiscriminately, but later they manage to compose stories. One boy typed very fast and said, "This is just like the truant officer does it."

Observation and Memory Activities. — Learning to observe and report their observations can help children who come to study centers. One standard activity is to display briefly a tray of objects. After it is removed, the children try to remember as many as they can. Since writing is hard and spelling is often poor, they may be encouraged to put down the beginning sounds of objects they remember. Then the group leader can write the list on paper or on the blackboard and see how many of them they can remember. Sometimes the children enjoy taking turns in describing a familiar object, giving one or two clues to start and adding clues until another child guesses.

"Concentration" can be played with any deck of cards or card game that has pairs of like cards. The cards are turned face down on a table. It may help to start with only a few pairs. One child turns up two cards. If they match, he keeps them and tries for another pair. When he misses, another child picks up two cards.

Reasoning and mathematical puzzles are popular. Children like to solve mazes and can learn to make them. Various types of maps can be used. A good beginning one is a map of the immediate neighborhood. Where is the study center, the school, their home, a friend's home, the church, the store, the stoplights, the trees? Mimeographed maps are nice to fill in and may be an activity continued for some time to watch for and locate new additions to the map.

Dictionary games are also made up by volunteers. What letters would I look under to find necklace, tiger, and so forth? How would our names be listed in alphabetical order? Sometimes one child suggests a letter and names something beginning with that letter. Each child adds a word beginning with the same letter.

Staff members often make homemade materials for learning. These include paper-plate clocks for learning to tell time and scrapbooks of categories of objects or pictures the child selects. Number books can also be made for small children by stapling ten sheets of paper into a booklet with a cover. It can be labeled "George's Number Book" or decorated to suit the child. The child can mark the pages with numbers from one to ten, and then draw or cut from a catalog three of something for the three page, and so on. Pictures of well-known people or places may be offered for the children to identify.

A rhyming game made up of twelve sets of four rhyming words printed on cards can be played according to the rules of the standard word game, "fish." Homemade lotto games can be made, using words or pictures that the children help to select. Cards of different colors can be printed with adjectives, nouns, verbs, adverbs, and pronouns — each part of speech on a separate color — and then arranged in piles to be read aloud.

In one center, none of the forty children involved had never played "hangman" before. Some of them had trouble finding words to use. One boy took a word from a book, forgot the page number, and did not know the word, so his game could not be solved. Another boy stumped the whole group with his unusual word, "coolmancool." A leader may suggest such categories as names of states (if a map is available), streets, baseball teams, or TV stars.

As part of the program of a study center, some games for amusement are appropriate. Such table games as checkers, dominoes, and bingo are used, if only for special events. The children often enjoy starting with a familiar game and learning new variations. Most of them have played checkers; many have never played "give-away." Most know the rules of basic bingo but have not played such variations as filling out a whole card, filling in the outline of a card, or forming letters such as "X" to win a game. In the same way, the familiar "Simon Says" may be used as "Mrs. Keller Says" or "Louis Says" if the children also need to learn the names of their staff and companions.

Volunteers often have hobbies and talents that are valuable. In one center a young man who knows magic tricks tutors a boy who is reluctant about reading. After each lesson the tutor demonstrates a magic trick and explains to the child how to do it. Then the boy does the trick.

The co-ordinator is responsible for seeing that materials and ideas for these activities are available. At times, children have good contributions, but it is unfair to expect them to assume a job of planning and direction that is basically the leader's job.

The adult leader will need to vary activities and develop some reasonable balance between active and quiet games. He may decide that the children need an active game. For example, in "Huckle-Buckle Beanstalk," a version of "Hide the Thimble," the children go out of the room and one person hides a thimble or small object — in plain sight. The children come in and hunt for it. As one sees it, he says, "Huckle-Buckle Beanstalk" and sits down. As the children find it, they each do the same until everyone is sitting down. This type of game is preferred for classrooms because everyone ends up in his chair. In planning activities, the adult has to think about what will follow, where the children will be physically when the game ends, and how transition to the next activity will be made.

The side benefits of study center activities have been impressive. Children have learned many leisure-time activities which they take home with them. Some have begun to visit each other's homes for the first time to play together and to continue activities that they learned in study centers.

V

Atmosphere and Resources

Volunteer work in education requires both an appropriate social setting as well as a physical location and teaching materials. There can be no doubt that the after-school study center emphasizes the proper climate in which teaching can take place. There are, of course, requirements for space, books, materials, and supplies, but these are minimum. With the increased availability of federal, local, and private sources of funds, the space problem is manageable. Creating the appropriate atmosphere is much more difficult.

ATMOSPHERE AND DISCIPLINE

The atmosphere of a study center or a tutoring project can range from the quiet and formality of a classroom to the informality of a social center. Most try to find a middle road. The school atmosphere — which often puts a premium on quiet — has not succeeded in motivating these children. A volunteer program should not be just another hour of school.

A study center is, ideally, a workshop for children where different activities go on at the same time. Quiet corners are needed for the work of tutors with individual children. In homework help, the children need freedom to move about and to talk to one another. Therefore, one can expect more conversation and noise in a study center than in a classroom. An effective classroom has interest corners where activities are available to children who have finished their work. The same procedure is required in a study center.

The sponsoring group should work toward a basic agreement about the kind of atmosphere they want to have. The co-ordinator has to make decisions about discipline after discussion with the sponsoring group. Volunteers must be oriented about their disciplinary responsibilities — and the limits to these responsibilities. Otherwise the children will be confused.

The children who come to study centers are generally as well behaved as any group of children. They are a select group who have accepted an offer of help. There must be an element of desire on their own part even though they are referred by the schools. If their only reason for coming is a parent's insistence, the parent has to be told that this is not a good basis for helping a child to learn. Often, of course, parents and teachers do encourage a child to come, and this may help to motivate the child for the first visit. After that, it is the responsibility of the staff to make the child, if not eager to come, at least tolerant. Parents may have to be assured that this is the task of the center.

Many of the children are self-disciplined and very capable in relating to both children and adults. Others have known mainly the extremes of adult behavior — either a lack of interest in helping them or an authoritarian and repressive approach to every issue. Their needs for power, self-respect, and participation are the same as those of any other child, but they may have had less experience in developing such skills. They need to make decisions that are theirs to make and to see responsible adults making decisions. They need to feel that they have some power over their own future. And, of course, the only worthwhile discipline is self-discipline.

In a group activity the discipline should come from the activity. The homework needs of the children imply a need for a degree of quiet (unlike study habits in some countries where children still study out loud with each child reciting his own lesson). Observation in study centers shows that the children do have impressive powers of concentration when they are genuinely interested in learning. Some do cherish the opportunity for more peace and quiet than they can find at home. So the atmosphere should be quiet enough to allow children to work, but the center should never enforce absolute quiet for its sake alone.

As the activities change, the discipline changes. Group games and dramatic activities do not need the same degree of quiet that homework and tutoring require. Unfortunately, some volunteer workers use these activities as a bribe, just as insensitive parents use dessert as a reward for eating a meal. The impression is, then, that vegetables or serious study are really intolerable — and these volunteers are downgrading what a study center has to offer. Actually, they should do just the opposite — make learning an attractive and rewarding experience.

Some volunteers are so afraid of helping children that they give up their adult roles or decide that games and fun are all the children want. Work with children who feel defeated in school may require patience, intellectual work in small doses, and frequent changes of pace. Those who participate do want to learn, however, and have a right to expect genuine academic help from study centers.

Children are very willing to understand consistent and reasonable adults. They can understand that the atmosphere is for the benefit of the majority of the group and not a matter of an adult's whim. The reaction of most children to a new setting is to see what it is like. It is impressive how much of the atmosphere of a place children seem to comprehend and respond to. They have a need to belong and a willingness to go along with reasonable adults. But if those adults order them to take their hats off, be quiet, or to indulge any of the other personal whims that adults like to pass off as their due as adults, the children will conform, but they will learn nothing except that adults push children around.

Any rules of a center, then, have to make sense. The first responsibility is for the physical safety of the children. If a child endangers himself or others, adults must react immediately and explain why. Unless there is a question of physical danger, the adult can ask himself why certain behavior bothers him. An adult's personal needs should not be satisfied by a study center for children.

In any group, individual and group needs can conflict. Obviously, the center has to serve groups of children, and no one child's needs can continually take precedence over those of the rest of the children. But the needs of these children for individual support and help are very great. If a program starts with trying to help too many children with too few adults, the needs of the children will not and cannot be met. The best answer is to have enough volunteers available.

Most children can explain their reactions if approached with patience. Certainly, unless an adult knows why and how trouble began, he can hardly decide on a solution. Putting himself in a child's place sometimes helps. An example is a boy who seemed very defensive and was always looking for a fight. Some members of a study center staff resented his attitude until they were told that his missing teeth and the scars on his head represented the brutal treatment he got at home. His defensiveness did not change for months, but their tolerance immediately increased. Instead of being considered a defensive kid looking for trouble, the boy became a challenge to prove that adults were worthy of trust and respect. This is an example where understanding of one child's situation helped in accepting him.

But study centers deal with groups — and difficulties between children can and do arise. If the volunteer does not know what happened, he asks. The tone of voice and attitude are more important than the words used. There are often two sides to a story, and the adult may be left still not knowing what happened. The children themselves may not even know, except for their own feelings. It is all right for the volunteer to say that he wants to believe them both, but if the only solution he can see is to separate them, he suggests that they each find someone with whom they can work happily. The main problem is to avoid over-reacting or making threats.

Some children want to know what the limits are, and an adult has to tell them. When the volunteer stops children from bothering others, he should tell them that he will not let them bother other children, nor will he let others bother them. The assurance that the adult will not let others bother a child is necessary and may be what the child really wants to know.

If a child has gotten along well before and suddenly becomes defiant or difficult, there is probably a reason. At least the adult should acknowledge this. He can say something like, "There must be something wrong." Sometimes privacy helps. If there is time for someone to walk over and sit with the child or to leave the room with him, he may be able to tell the adult what is wrong. He may not. It is important that the volunteer offer help: "I wish you'd tell me what it's all about." If the child cannot, he should be assured that if he wants to talk later, the adult will be there. Often a child relates to some staff member because he is the one who has given the child something and can therefore ask about the child's problem. Obviously, a volunteer who does not know a child should not be put into the spot of trying to help in a crisis. The co-ordinator or the volunteer who works closely with a child is the reasonable one for the child to confide in. Other adults cannot expect the same trust.

Adults often create their own problems in a study center, just as they do in any work with children. An unusual example is the volunteer who had a child come for a first lesson with a bottle of perfume to sell to her. She wondered what to tell the boy when he asked if she would buy it, and the incident was prolonged until she asked the study center co-ordinator what to do. She was told to say the obvious, "No, but I will help you with your reading," and then do it.

A sense of fair play and a sense of humor both help with children. Humor should never be used to hurt children, but the ability to laugh at oneself is a virtue. Children like to know that adults are human and do not have all the answers. It may be best to pass off an incident with a remark such as, "No, I don't know what's wrong but if no one feels that it is an earth-shaking problem, I have a story I think you will enjoy." Later, if the adult feels that a child is still deeply concerned about an incident, he may want to talk to those concerned. Children have a great capacity to differ with another child and later to seek out the same child for a game. They also are the first to suggest that adults not make a federal case out of a perfectly healthy disagreement.

Many study centers have a list of rules, usually made up by the staff. It would seem obvious that the more reasonable and brief such rules are, the better. At one study center, the staff and children composed the rules. The children wanted a rule about obeying adults, but the staff explained that a study center is not an army base. Was there a better word than "obey"? The children finally suggested, "Be kind to tutors," which seems appropriate. In their discussions the children were told that rules should have a reason behind them. Therefore, Rule 6 on their list reads, "Do not put your coat on the floor." Rule 7 states, "Because someone might step on it." This group, which included several pre-delinquents, felt that fighting was out of place in a study center. They also ruled out messing around. When asked to explain the difference, they made the point that fighting is two-sided. Messing around or "bugging" is one-sided—the pestering of one child by another. Children have a right to expect adult protection from either form of aggression, even if they started the trouble. They may need to be told how they caused the trouble, and respect for their feelings may make it worthwhile for the adult to explain this in private. At this study center, the children now realize how long it takes to compose satisfactory rules.

Any set of rules should probably be considered a crutch for the staff, to be used if necessary to help define the atmosphere of a new center. Unfortunately, such rules may then become the basis of authority, when the actual authority should be the adult in charge. The real reason for stopping undesirable behavior, of course, is not that it is against the rules, but that it is just not acceptable to an adult whose job is to teach the children in his care. To hide behind rules is to fail in assuming an adult role.

Explanations about why certain behavior is unacceptable should be brief and explicit. If children ask why they can't do something and the real reason is "because I won't let you," there is no need to say more. Some children do have to test the limits. They may have to find out that the volunteer means what he says. So the adult must be sure himself and must explain the limits or the reasonable consequences of the child's behavior.

Some days there may be a shortage of volunteers or of ideas—or nothing seems to work. Then a child who is not able to benefit

from the study center that day may be told to leave and return
tomorrow or for his next regular appointment. This is not a
solution, but an expedient which may be necessary in terms of
helping a group of children.

The best atmosphere in any classroom or study center is a
reasonable combination of freedom and order. A study center
can offer freedom to talk, to walk around, and to select activities
and materials. But order is necessary too, since freedom by itself
is not a basis for group activity. When one child's freedom im-
poses on another's, then a responsible adult may have to inter-
vene. The point of intervention can only be decided in terms
of a knowledge of the children involved. Of course, the adult in
authority should be one whom the children know and respect.
It is helpful for adults to accept the idea that they have to give
something before expecting any return from a child. If adults
have been fair and reasonable in their requests and have not
had to assert continually their adult authority, the payoff will
come when there is real need for intervention.

There is basic consensus against the use of physical force with
children in volunteer work. It seems obvious that an adult hitting
a child could only demonstrate that adults have no self-control.
On rare occasions, however, study center personnel have to ask
a child to leave because they cannot tolerate his type of behavior.

Adults who display consistent, fair, and responsible behavior
are the chief examples in demonstrating to children what the
centers want of them. That these adults work together with
mutual respect is equally important. There will also be opportunities to extend the same respect to the teachers and parents
of the children. With this basis of mutual respect, study centers
can contribute to children's efforts to develop a reasonable, co-
herent view of the world.

COMPETITION AND STANDARDS OF BEHAVIOR

Volunteers in educational work must be prepared to deal with
children who have a wide variation in their standards of personal behavior. The atmosphere of the study center or the tutoring project is designed to help the volunteer make a good contact

with the youngsters. The volunteer must be sensitive to the needs of the children and still recognize the impact that the family and school have had.

Often these children reveal that competition has failed to operate as a basis for developing positive motivation and an interest in learning. Therefore, one of the advantages of individual work with children is that the need for competition with other children is reduced. In the one-to-one relationship of tutoring, the child is much less concerned with what other children are doing and more concerned with the progress of his own work. When study centers work with groups of children, however, competition becomes an issue.

Children of all ability levels often seem unduly concerned with showing what they can do. They need to show their abilities, but adults must try to be aware of what competition does to them. Those who are capable want to demonstrate their superiority, and those who are less able often demand contests which seem self-defeating, since they always lose.

Children should be told that a study center is a place where each child can get the help he needs. If volunteers are interested in the achievement of individual children, there will be opportunities to demonstrate this interest. If a volunteer is honestly more interested in what a child does this week compared to his performance last week than in what Mary Jones or anyone else does, he will find opportunities to say so.

The adult's words about competition, however, will mean far less to the children than his behavior. How he chooses to use activities and games will reveal his own conviction that their individual needs are what is important. Most children's games are based on competition, but a volunteer can change them if he likes. If a game calls for children to be eliminated when they miss an answer, he may change the rules. Too often the children who need the play experience most are the ones who would be left out, whereas others are able to continually show their superiority in one specific skill. The adult can also praise effort or improvement and avoid criticism and comparative judgment.

Children who insist on fierce competition with others sometimes feel a need to prove what they can do. At the other extreme are those among the least capable who continually want to compete, as if to confirm their own low opinion of themselves. They both need help. The superior students may need to be told, "Yes, you are good in arithmetic." The others need to be recognized and encouraged as much as the superior students.

Sometimes children want adults to mark their papers. Volunteers have tried putting 100's, colored stars, smiling faces, or OK's on the children's papers. Since a study center is not a school, volunteers do not have to engage in these practices. Instead, children can be encouraged to bring stories and drawings to be put on the bulletin board. Their individual writing is sometimes marked with comments about the writing, without comparative judgments. It is better if treats rather than prizes are given to all children.

Another potential area of competition involves the distribution of magazines or booklets to the children. Until the children are able to accept the fact that they really are treated as individuals, it would be best to make sure that there are enough magazines so that each child can be given one. At first, their need may be so great that they are really unable to make a meaningful choice. In one center, it took some months for the children to learn that the staff was consistent. Boys were given popular science magazines, and some children who needed help with handwriting were given booklets on handwriting. When several girls asked if they could have the same, it was explained that different children get different things according to their interests and what the staff felt could help them. The little girls were offered fashion magazines the next day and were delighted. Later they brought back the paper dolls they had made. After the children learned to accept the intentions of the adults, they were in a better position to make their own selections.

The same concern with competition is one of the problems that parents most often discuss. If the volunteer explains a child's individual abilities, many parents can understand that it is unfair to compare their child continually with another. It may help them accept the volunteer's ideas if he points out that we do not expect one housewife to bake delicious cakes just because her

sister does, but we sometimes forget that children are also individuals.

When children are under more pressure to compete than they
can tolerate or when they feel unsure of their own abilities, they
tend to cheat. In the long run, the school and volunteer workers
must prepare them for the realities of adult life, but inside the
study center it is not necessary to be punitive. Such behavior
should be discouraged and the pressures that lead to it gradually
eliminated. It is the atmosphere of the study center and not a
specific set of rules that helps to overcome cheating.

RESOURCES AND MATERIALS

Physical space requirements vary, but should be decided in
terms of the number of children involved in a program. The
number of different activities that can be conducted in a small
space is impressive. As an extreme example, in one small storefront, approximately 10 by 15 feet, 40 children work at small
tables. In one corner, a volunteer distributes mimeographed
books and the children read aloud. Three feet away other groups
are engaged in other activities.

For individual help, partitions and small tables such as card
tables give an important element of privacy. For a more general
program, the availability of two rooms increases flexibility. Often
children do their homework or receive tutoring help in one room
and then go to another room for educational games or activities.
The lack of a separate activity room makes it difficult to develop
a flexible program. Discussion groups also need some privacy.

In a storefront space that totals 18 by 70 feet, a library room in
front serves approximately 400 children who often come only
for library books. Four reading tables are available. In the back
room, eight individual booths provide space for tutoring, and
three large tables are available for homework help. About 50
children use part of these facilities daily.

Legal responsibility for the safety and well-being of the children while on the premises of the study center will depend upon
local laws. The basic need is liability insurance which is usually

included in the cost of the rent. Every group should make certain that they are adequately covered in this respect. If there is any doubt, legal advice should be obtained.

Equipment for most volunteer centers has usually been donated. Besides tables and chairs, low shelves for books, a desk for records, and possibly a file cabinet, the biggest need is for books. Even if a public library is near, such materials as encyclopedias — preferably ones the children can read, dictionaries, and a globe are necessary. Phonics and reading-exercise workbooks are needed by the staff. In some centers, these are used with thin tracing paper so that they can be used later by other children. Since they are often used as review or as supplementary material, tutors like the flexibility of using specific exercises without using an entire workbook. Bulletin boards are important and can be made of cardboard or burlap. Blackboards are most useful and have been made with blackboard paint.

Centers usually try to provide a variety of materials available for the use of both the volunteers and the children. Some volunteers have a mistaken idea that these materials should all be new and different from what is used in school. Many children want the familiar materials which may represent the only books they have read successfully. They often ask for something they know, and many of them especially want readers. Old readers have been cut up and made into reading units so that the children are able to complete a story and feel the accomplishment of finishing an assignment. There is no doubt that big books often seem overwhelming to the children, but sometimes they can be encouraged to choose specific stories that appeal to them.

Easy reading books for young children and controlled vocabulary books for older readers are especially needed. Books about Negro children and their heroes such as Abraham Lincoln, John Kennedy, and Martin Luther King are important. Nonsense and rhyme are so in demand that Dr. Seuss is standard. One center in a poor neighborhood has his books chained to a table as its most cherished possession.

Study centers have an advantage in being able to offer materials that are new and are not yet used in the school curriculum.

This is especially true of the new city-oriented readers that are being published.

For a long time all ethnic minorities were ignored in school texts. Educators have for years complained about the lack of Negro children in school books. The children's reaction to library books and readers that picture Negro children is impressive. It is exciting to them, and they often comment with surprise and pleasure. The fact that some of the new materials show a little emotion and that not all the faces are always smiling seems important, too. The content is sometimes more poetic than earlier materials and the activities of the characters more appealing.

The advantage of standard reading materials, however, is that everyone can share the common dreams and wishes they represent. The value of reading about families that are intact and people who have exciting adventures is that children identify with the story and vicariously share these experiences.

In the development of new materials, realism about city life should not lose all the values of vicarious enjoyment. There is now great interest in developing special materials for deprived children. No material can be good for deprived children unless it is good for all children. We cannot afford to further alienate these youngsters by denying them the right to share the same dreams and hopes of other children. A culturally ghettoized curriculum would destroy the opportunity to bring them into the mainstream of American life. If they need more active experiences in learning, as many authorities feel they do, this is no different from the needs of all other children who spend too much time in passive learning, being quietly bored.

Since the good library books in which the characters happen to be Negro have been published recently, they are not usually received as donations. Centers usually have to plan some special funds for these. They should not be labeled "brotherhood" books or kept in a special category. They are as important to white children as they are to Negro youngsters. Any of us would resent having books about our national origin labeled as special — as if such materials were being consciously used to help others tolerate us. New material should be judged not simply on the basis of its use of Negro or Oriental faces, but rather on its value as literature.

The children themselves often select the materials that appeal to them. An assortment of pictures of white and Negro children were offered for story-telling. The Negro children often selected pictures of white children. A picture of a white child and father was selected by a Negro girl, who started her story, "I am reading to my daddy."

Consumable supplies include library materials, paper and pencils, washroom supplies, and postcards to communicate with families who have no phone. Quantities of scrap paper are used and can be obtained as donations. Children often need writing paper or pencils, and these are a continuing expense.

Some provision should be made for after-school snacks for study centers in deprived areas. In general, projects have found that children arrive from school hungry. This is particularly relevant for tutoring work, since hunger interferes with achievement and interest. Snacks should be provided by the center budget and should not be used as a bribe or as a reward. These snacks usually consist of crackers, cookies, or fruit, which are preferable to candy and gum. In one center in the inner city, fresh fruit is the biggest treat in the eyes of the children.

USE OF THE PUBLIC LIBRARY

If there is a public library near a study center, individual tutors will use it with individual children, or groups of children can be taken there by volunteers. Middle-class parents have experience in running interference in libraries for their children. No one will do this for the lower-class child unless volunteers do. Teachers often encourage their children and sometimes help them in getting cards but many inner city children do not use public libraries.

A staff member should visit the library and know what the facilities are and the hours of operation. He should get cards for the children so that they can have help in filling them out, getting their parents' signatures, and getting identification to prove residency, if required. He should explain to the children what a library is and the kind of behavior that is expected there. With a properly filled-out card the children can take out a book the first time they go, which is much better than to take them there only to start the process of getting a card. Unfortunately, some libraries still believe in guilt by association so that if any member of a family owes a fine, no other member of the family can take out a book. If this should be the case, the fines should be paid. Getting the card is not enough. The children must be taken to the library at regularly scheduled opportunities. They will need help in finding books they can read. Sometimes they can be encouraged to take books below their level which they can really read. They may use the excuse of reading to younger siblings. Unfortunately, many librarians, both in the schools and public libraries, have taken a course which taught them what children should read at certain ages. They often tell good readers that a book is "too hard for you," although the child may have read it five times. This is no problem for the middle-class child who comes home, laughs about the experience, and asks his mother to get the book, knowing that she will. Eventually, of course, we would hope that the children would use the library on their own, but until they do, it should be planned, if possible, to escort them for a long time.

CULTURAL ENRICHMENT

There is, naturally, concern with the lack of cultural stimulation in the lives of inner city children. Any center that tries to help children academically will be questioned about its interests and efforts in this direction.

The experience of coming to a center and meeting adequate, interested adults is in itself a good social experience. Volunteers have a unique opportunity to find subjects and materials to stimulate the children's interest and offer enrichment in a meaningful way.

There is nothing enriching in and of itself in exposing a child to various media, as the following illustration shows. An after-school center wanted to offer a special activity during the holidays. A volunteer therefore made homemade clay and brought it in for the children to use. She also brought materials to work with such as rolling pins, kitchen utensils, and cookie cutters. The children did not know what to do with the clay and tended to copy the work of a few children who had ideas. The children enjoyed the activity, but the volunteer felt that it was not developed in a meaningful way.

Later, at the same center a teacher of a reading club brought in homemade clay so that the children could make their favorite story book characters. She had introduced them to a large variety of characters through her reading to them and through their individual reading selections. The result was that the children eagerly used the clay to make representations of their favorite characters. The two experiences illustrate that material may be considered cultural or useful, but may be enriching only when it relates to an interest of the children.

A study center need make no apologies for its inability to afford elaborate activities outside of the center. With luck in recruiting volunteers, there will be an abundance of available resources that can be stimulating and rewarding. In fact, one purpose of these centers is to develop worthwhile ways of using leisure time, and it would be a disservice to give children the idea that only by driving across the city or spending a lot of money can one enjoy a cultural experience.

Individual tutors will also become interested in the needs of individual children and may offer them special outings, according to their interests. Later on, a group may be able to organize volunteers for occasional trips. It is best when such activities involve a group of people who know each other and have some shared background and experience. This kind of program, therefore, could best develop out of others.

In planning trips, it is important that there be a volunteer available for every five to eight children, depending upon the children's ages and the skill of the volunteers. Permission must be obtained from the parents and insurance and finances considered. One advantage of trips in the city is that children often do not know what is available to them. After visits to museums and parks with volunteers, the children return there with their families and friends.

To avoid concern with personal liability and driving ability, it is better to use public transportation. Another good reason for this is that centers are educating children about their own city. After one trip for which private cars were used, a little boy said, "My mother would sure like to see this museum, but she can't come. She hasn't got a car." Nearly every child in the inner city can afford bus fare for a trip. Parents are generally so grateful for the chance for their children to have outings that they are willing to pay the fare.

VI

Volunteers

RECRUITMENT

The effectiveness of a study center depends basically upon its volunteers. In an economically mixed area, personnel resources are more readily available. In poorer neighborhoods, the number of available qualified volunteers is much smaller. In such areas, programs often begin with the extensive involvement of professional teachers. For example, teachers meet with groups of children in a setting that is clearly another hour of school. In other instances volunteers are bussed in. New projects often start out using only one source of volunteers. One used only housewives supplied by a service league, another only college students, and a third only high school students. Most gradually expand their recruitment efforts, after realizing that no one group is uniquely qualified to give volunteer help.

The largest single source of volunteer help is college and university students. They have the optimism of youth — that problems can be solved, the glamor of their position — young adults still close to the children in age, and the prestige of going to college. Many inner city children have not known a college student before.

Possibly because they have been so active in the field of volunteer tutoring, we know more of their difficulties than we do of other groups of volunteers. One problem is their heavy schedule of academic and non-academic activities. Another is that young people who are trying to free themselves from parents can and do get their own needs for independence confused with the needs of the children. It would be wrong to assume that college students cannot do a job because of their own needs for independence. But it would be equally wrong not to realize that these years represent a striving for independence that often expresses itself in exaggerated hostility to the square institutions and people who are seen as standing in the way of progress. Those projects involving college students that have the sympathetic participation of faculty members often maintain good morale.

Sometimes the sincere concern of college students and young adults to contribute also makes them dissatisfied with their own work. They often feel a need to see results sooner than do older volunteers. If their dissatisfaction is communicated to the child, he may wonder whether he can ever achieve.

In depressed areas, high school students are often one of the few available groups and are being successfully recruited. These students are near the age of the children needing help and represent successful growing up. Whether they are paid should depend upon their need. Although the status and work experience may constitute the reward, financial payment may be essential.

There has been less experience in study centers in using children from the upper elementary grades. Older school children have helped younger children in schools ever since the public school system developed. There may be two special reasons why more efforts ought to be made to use those in seventh and eighth grades, for example, to help study center children. One is the strong sibling relationships in lower-class families. The other is that seventh and eighth grade achievement represents a realizable goal for these children, and they need such goals. Children who have graduated from tutoring have often absorbed much of the attitude of the staff, and they are sometimes interested and able to help other children.

Men have a special appeal, of course, since there are not enough men in the lives of many of these children. In addition, the demonstration that learning is a manly activity can be particularly helpful. Elementary schools are women-oriented. Girls need the image of helpful, interested men as much as the boys do. It would be foolish to recruit or exclude any specific group,

however. Women have the know-how and more opportunities
to work with children since, in our society, so much of the task
of educating children has traditionally been their job.

Retired adults are also active in projects. When they have
worked successfully with children, they lend a sense of security
to which children respond well. And when they are effective,
they make an enormous contribution, both to the inexperienced
volunteers and to the children. It is impressive how the toughest
and oldest youngsters will often seek out a gray-haired adult, as
if sensing that here is someone who will not be too concerned
by his poor achievement and who may be able to help him.

Both active and retired teachers are heavily involved in tutoring and study center projects. They are often the ones to whom
other volunteers turn for help with books and materials.

Regardless of the background of the volunteer, it is important
that he start with the interests of the children. Perhaps an example will illustrate this point. A teen-age girl came to a volunteer
for academic help. The girl said she saw no use in reading. The
volunteer, accepting the judgment as valid or at least as a pretty
definite statement of lack of interest, said, "Would you like to
learn to knit?" The girl immediately said yes and learned to
knit and to follow simple directions in a knitting book. After
several lessons, the girl began to explore the books the tutor had
available on the table—which she had not pushed on the girl.
The girl began to read, not because the knitting led to reading
but because someone had accepted her and given her something
she wanted with no strings attached. Theoretically, an experienced teacher could do the same thing, but if she rigidly followed
her training in teaching reading, she might feel compelled to
approach the child as a reading problem.

In recruiting volunteers, it is important to stress the supportive
nature of their work. The greatest challenge in the use of volunteers is to develop realistic goals. Their goals have to be the reasonable ones that can be expected from a short-term volunteer
commitment. In one case, a child asked a volunteer to write in
his autograph book. The adult wrote, "To Mike — in hopes that
you will go to college." The child read it, looked up at the adult,
and said, "You mean you hope I'll learn to read better." The

child's goal was realistic; that of the adult, pretentious. The child was saying, "Don't push me. I'm trying to read better. That's what I can attempt now." Whether a 10-year-old child who is retarded in reading should be encouraged to go to college is not a proper judgment for a volunteer.

Education is and will remain basically the task of the schools. Volunteers in education are not expected to be reading teachers, nor are they expected to know elaborate remedial techniques. They are expected to build on the efforts of the school. If volunteers work in opposition to either the home or the school, they can only contribute to a child's difficulties. He does not need a figure of authority who wants to compete with either his parents or his teacher for his loyalty.

Some volunteers have been taken in by children wanting to impress or shock them. One child told elaborate stories of beatings in his school. It never occurred to the volunteer to ask someone about the story. If he had visited the school, he would have known better, but instead he became very concerned and hostile to the school authorities. Children sometimes report about their homes in the same way, including wishful tales about possessing three television sets or large bookcases full of books. It is not always necessary to express doubt, but it is important to remember that children can and do test out adults.

Unfortunately, volunteers are sometimes oversold on the value of their contribution. We ought to have more appreciation of the value of their work than to feel it necessary to oversell. The rewards are genuine. But if volunteers are told only of the successes and the unusual academic gains that a few children make, they will have unrealistic expectations.

The disabilities of the children who use study centers have taken years to develop. It would be unreasonable to expect quick cures from the efforts of volunteers working one hour a week. If a project has some stability through a paid staff member or volunteers who remain with the project for a year or two, they will see more long-term achievements. Volunteers will understand their job better if given a realistic view of their potential contribution. A child's reading score may not go up one-tenth of a percentage point, but his attitude, as observed by his teacher and tutor, may change. This is a valid achievement which can be realized in a semester. In fact, since we know that without help these children would continue to fall behind, it should be pointed out that to maintain their present level or a normal rate of gain may already represent an achievement.

In one effective tutoring project, both the co-ordinator and the school authorities help in orienting new volunteers. They are told that reading scores may not improve but that their contributions can be meaningful in other ways. The result is that academic gains are signs of extra achievement, and volunteers do not feel pushed to achieve in only one area. Without realistic objectives, volunteers may drop out or complain that all they are doing is contributing a little to improving race relations.

How are volunteers recruited? By word-of-mouth, notices in stores, and stories in local newspapers. Projects that have used various means of recruiting feel that word-of-mouth is the most important single method. Volunteers who do a meaningful job tend to recruit others who can do a good job. Recruitment should not be the job of the volunteers, but they often share their experiences and enthusiasm with neighborhood and civic groups. Hearing about the job from an experienced volunteer is reassuring to potential volunteers.

ORIENTATION AND SUPERVISION

Whoever the volunteers are and whatever their backgrounds, they all need some orientation and supervision. At the beginning of a semester or a school year when new volunteers are recruited, a group orientation meeting should be planned. Volunteers need to know the general and specific goals of a project. They want to know something about the children who come to the center, their families, and their school backgrounds. Orientation materials, records of the center, and the responsibilities of volunteers should be explained. The school referral form on the individual child is an important part of this information. Volunteers want to know who is in charge of the center and to whom they can turn for help. What length of commitment is expected from them? What is the procedure for reporting attendance and non-attendance of children? Whom do they call if unable to keep an appointment? What is the center's policy on contacts with schools and homes? What is the procedure for taking children on outings?

Most projects have volunteers joining the staff at various times. Often the co-ordinator or a designated volunteer has to assume the job of orienting new volunteers who join throughout the year. It helps to have a written statement of basic orientation available or a kit of materials. There should also be a shelf of books, pamphlets, and articles available for volunteers to check out and read.

In basic orientation, questions about the safety of a neighborhood usually arise. These must be answered honestly, and thought must be given to where volunteers will park, where telephones are available, and what provisions are made to escort women to their cars if they desire such assurance. If safety is a concern of volunteers, they can be assured by the experiences of former volunteers. But they should be encouraged to come with friends if they are genuinely concerned, even if their concern is considered unfounded. It is much easier to go with a friend who shares the walk or drive and with whom one can plan and share experiences.

There is a much more important reason for encouraging participation of volunteers by pairs or groups. Teaching is a lonely profession compared to others. (It is ironic how many articles are written about the lonely housewife, isolated with small children for hours every day. Teachers often live in the same isolation from adults, but little is written about it.)

Some record should be made of what a volunteer feels his or her commitment can be. These record forms vary, but usually contain basic information about the time available, the experience of the person offering his services as a volunteer, and something about his desires concerning the type of work that he feels he can do best.

It is good if the sponsoring agency can have a variety of jobs available that are known to the person recruiting volunteers. There may be volunteers who do not appear to relate well to other people, but who could be encouraged to join in work parties and do more routine jobs. It is also good if the volunteers can be asked to visit the center so that the person in charge can get some opinion of their ability. Some people automatically choose routine jobs and feel most comfortable in them. This may include working on materials, secretarial work, checking books out to children or processing books, or minding a paperback book store. This does not mean that these routine jobs are not important and that these people cannot also become crucial to the children. The shy or reserved volunteer who begins in one of these routine jobs often learns to relate to the children, particularly if he is helped by the supervisor. To be able to seat one child at the desk near an adult may relieve a difficult situation at the study table and may help to show volunteers how they can begin to have more of a role in working with the children.

Volunteers in any project are expected to make a firm commitment of time, usually for a minimum of one semester. Since the centers work with children who have been disappointed before in their expectations of learning and who come voluntarily for help, volunteers must understand the need for consistency. Although the job is a volunteer one, the commitment is professional. The children have a right to expect that their volunteer will attend regularly and be on time. The reaction of the children to an absence often shows how much this experience means to them. When a volunteer was late, a child said with relief, "I thought you were never coming back."

Volunteers usually agree to work one afternoon or evening a week. There are exceptions. One volunteer comes each week to a center on her day off and is a general helper. Since her day off comes on a different day each week, she is unable to accept a specific assignment. Occasionally, a volunteer can only come once in two weeks but is willing to help wherever needed. Individual tutoring requires at least a once-a-week assignment, but there ought to be enough flexibility to use available talent if using it will not disrupt the program. Volunteers also give demonstrations for special occasions which may be a one- or two-hour contribution.

In the selection of volunteers, abilities to relate to children are more important than academic training. Someone — usually the co-ordinator — has to assume responsibility for observing new volunteers and deciding that the person's work is satisfactory. Groups of people have been recruited and then have been let down by finding that the facilities were not ready. In any project it should be someone's responsibility to see that the volunteers have a job to do. If there are books to be processed and materials to be gotten ready, at least this will show the volunteers that they are appreciated and needed. They can be asked to visit once, but cannot be expected to visit a project for weeks while waiting for an assignment.

New volunteers should be encouraged to start with one child even if they feel that they can probably do more. Overenthusiasm often causes a new volunteer to want to offer a lot of service. Many volunteers regularly give two afternoons a week, but in general, the enthusiastic ones who offer several days a week are often unaware of the work involved and quickly become discouraged. It is better to encourage an undercommitment of time at first and then expand the hours as the volunteer realizes what the job involves.

Initial enthusiasm is relatively easy to get because of the appeal of a new program. After the initial enthusiasm wanes, the real test of a project is how much continuous, supportive help the volunteers receive. They need someone to answer their questions on a day-to-day basis and someone to help them find appropriate books and materials.

Ongoing supervision of volunteers is of two forms. First, the study center co-ordinator seeks to work with and help tutors by making suggestions and having informal conferences. Often projects have an experienced tutor on duty each day who can act as a resource person. The staff will feel more secure if there is someone to whom they can turn for an immediate answer to their questions.

Second, study centers and tutoring projects hold periodic staff conferences as an effective means of supervision. At these conferences, visiting experts can give professional guidance. Sometimes these visitors come from a cooperating school or a nearby college or university. More often, a volunteer teacher, active or retired, or the study center co-ordinator leads a group discussion in which common problems are explored. There are no fixed rules for holding these meetings, and they should not be made obligatory or cumbersome. But such staff conferences can meet important needs of the volunteers who, as they start out, have no basis for judging the success of their efforts. It offers an opportunity for them to express their feelings about their work. A sense of comradeship is reinforced at these meetings. Volunteers are all busy people, however, and cannot be expected to attend more than one discussion meeting a month. Even this may have to be planned at the end of lessons on a specific evening and rotated to meet different schedules.

One project that tutors ninety children has four resource people available — experienced tutors or teachers — to whom the volunteers can turn for help. They can choose their own supervisor but have to make the arrangements outside of center hours at their mutual convenience. This works well in a middle-class neighborhood. In other neighborhoods, volunteers travel a distance to work and it is better to have provisions for help the evening they come to the center. Either the co-ordinator has to be trained to help them, or other resource people must be available.

MAINTAINING A VOLUNTEER STAFF

Concern is sometimes expressed about the kinds of volunteers who may not be satisfactory. Such questions are usually asked by professionals who have generally been slow in developing ways of using non-professionals in our society. The motives of volunteers are of importance to these people. Some project recruiters ask volunteers why they want to help. Others consider this an invasion of privacy and prefer only to see if the prospective volunteer has something to offer. The answers to why volunteers want to work seem to be an expression of the widespread concern and knowledge about our educational problems. Occasionally, a very personal reason is given such as "I was a school-leaver myself and have always regretted it." Generally, the discovery of the disadvantaged in our society has led to both renewed interest and willingness to help. After meeting hundreds of volunteers, we see no need to question their motives, any more than we would question the motives of youngsters who come for help. Their coming to a center means that they want help. The attendance of volunteers obviously shows that they want to help.

What about those volunteers who cannot fit into a program? There are not many people who wish to work with children on a regular basis who cannot be helped to do a useful job. It helps to have a variety of jobs available so that some persons can be assigned as general helpers if there is doubt about their ability to relate to children.

Obviously, those mentally disturbed or disorganized individuals who are more often attracted by mass appeals should be screened out. Newspaper and television appeals seem to bring some of these, which is another reason why word of mouth is preferred as a recruitment method. There are few of these persons, however, and their defects are obvious even to nonprofessional directors of projects. These people are talked with briefly and told that they will be called when needed. They are usually not heard of again.

More of a problem are those volunteers who seem unable to work with other adults. These include the loud and boisterous, the inveterate gum-chewer, and those who interfere in the work of other adults. For the benefit of the whole staff, they may have to be asked not to come again.

The jobs that volunteers do, of course, vary tremendously. Anyone unwilling to come regularly or to give some nominal report of his work is not effective and may be asked to leave. Although convinced that most volunteers could learn to make a contribution if given enough help, projects sometimes have to decide that some volunteers are not worth the time necessary to help them. The contribution to a child or a group is not worth the continual support they need. Many projects subtly drop these volunteers by not calling them back the next semester.

The ability of projects to hold their volunteers may vary as much as their ability to keep children interested in a program. If volunteers make a commitment to a project and then do not keep it, their reasons ought to be explored. In one instance, volunteers left near the end of a semester, each giving a valid explanation of other commitments. During the next year, the same volunteers came back saying that word had reached them that the project was now organized in a meaningful way. They really wanted to help, but their concern with the disorganization of the previous year had led them to decide that their work was not worthwhile. In another instance, the main reason for staff dissatisfaction and withdrawal from the program was the co-ordinator's habit of ordering volunteers about and his detached attitude toward their work.

Sometimes efforts to attract and keep volunteers are defeated by the needs of the larger agency which sponsors the project. If names of volunteers are used by other groups for fund-raising, the volunteers will naturally resent it. Neither should they be expected to give help in collecting materials for the center. If money and materials are a concern of a center, as they often are, a separate citizens' group of volunteers can be developed.

RECOGNITION

All agencies using volunteers have methods of recognition. Study centers and tutoring projects usually use luncheons or evening meetings with guest speakers. Volunteers should also receive a thank-you letter at the end of the semester. This would seem obvious but represents a common complaint, since most projects handle the recognition of volunteers on a mass basis. Often a personalized letter would be more appreciated than a mimeographed invitation to a group gathering.

Volunteers need to be recognized and thanked by being told that they are appreciated. A co-ordinator has to say this often. not just to feel it. Such statements as "We really count on you," "I'll see you next week," or just plain "Thank you for your help" are apparently not said often enough. Volunteers want to feel needed and useful, and many of them need assurance that they are.

Appreciation of volunteers can be shown in many other ways. A group of high-school youngsters began to help in two centers, both located in churches. Volunteer attendance in one church was excellent; the other had very low participation. One visit from a consulting staff member revealed the reason. In the first church, the minister opened his apartment to the students when they arrived. They had tea with him and discussed current events. The children being tutored began to arrive half an hour later. In the second, no effort was made to welcome the tutors. A common complaint of these volunteers was, "No one knew I was there." These high school youngsters, like all other volunteers, needed to know that someone was aware of their contribution.

USING CHILDREN AS HELPERS

Without any prompting from adults, children often offer help to other children in a study center. Every good teacher uses children in the class as helpers. Because of the relaxed atmosphere in an after-school study center, there are many opportunities to let children help. The children naturally want to be like the adults they admire, and their self-respect and confidence can be enhanced by their feelings of being helpful.

One of the easiest ways to let children help is to have them read to younger children. Girls often complain about not getting enough opportunities to read out loud in school. They may need an adult to listen to them at first before they are willing to read out loud to children. Because a child reads well does not mean that she can read to a group without encouragement. But their need to read out loud may be welcomed if there is a group who could benefit from a story. The adult may assume responsibility in helping to select a story, and see that the children are comfortable and listening.

Many boys who come for reading help are good in arithmetic. If a child is struggling with the multiplication tables, a volunteer may ask another child who is good in arithmetic to help. "I need your help. Could you please write out the times tables of two for Nancy?" Chances are the child will not only write they out, but he may offer to help the other child learn them or to write some more later when she needs them.

Children may also help in running the library. These jobs must make sense to both the adult and the child, however.

An adult who thinks he is using a clever gimmick and fooling a child is only belittling him, and the child knows it.

It may take more time for children to help than for adults to do the job. This is true of the normal help that parents encourage their children to give. For many children whose parents do not have the time or the skill to let them help, these experiences are important. Of course, a volunteer must know the children, their capabilities, and his own ability to accept what they do.

In establishing one new center, children helped in cleaning up and painting. They collected and processed books and distributed flyers. One Saturday, after washing the windows of the storefront center, they went up and down the block asking for and receiving permission to wash all the windows on the block. After the center opened, the children continued to help by arranging books in order, checking books in and out, and participating with the staff in clean-up days. If adults are willing to work with children instead of assigning them jobs, the children enjoy the task more. They may gradually be able to work alone, but still need assurance and recognition.

Sometimes adults have become discouraged by their attempts to let children help. In one center in a deprived area, some boys were asked to put chairs in a circle. They did so but first dumped children sitting on them onto the floor. Some staff members seemed ready to say, "We told you so — they can't help." These people had probably never visited a middle-class youth group to observe how many children behave irresponsibly when first given authority. All children have to be taught how to help. Over-control or neglect are both easy ways to deal with children, but teaching is a human experience that assumes a capacity to give and to learn.

It may become desirable to pay some children for their help. If there are a lot of eligible helpers, the jobs can be rotated. Payment can also be in the form of a scholarship to an after-school sports activity or to a dramatics, music, or art center. The ability to be on time and to do a creditable job, plus the opportunity to manage money, is another worthwhile part of education that some of these children need.

VII

Results and Effectiveness

The goals of tutoring programs and after-school study centers
are many. Volunteer workers seek to uncover new interests in
underachieving youngsters, to establish meaningful relations
with them out of which new attitudes and stronger motives
for learning can emerge, and to help them master basic academic skills. Any method of evaluation of these efforts must
be broadly conceived and realistically and carefully designed.

It will not be possible to evaluate the efforts of most groups.
Systematic evaluation of after-school study centers requires the
efforts of trained researchers. A program as bold and as ex-
perimental as the after-school center movement will have to
push ahead and make mistakes. The vital forces at work cannot permit premature or hostile evaluation to stop the efforts
of communities to help themselves.

MATERIALS FOR EVALUATION

The most dramatic evaluation is for an observer to visit a
study center. One has only to observe the excitement and the
range of activities and the willingness of youngsters to use these
facilities to realize that the experience is an immediately valid
one. However formal or informal the atmosphere, children are
exposed to interested, helpful young people and adults of different backgrounds. By attending a center, children choose
to spend their free time in learning activities.

Nevertheless, every study center can collect some material that is useful for evaluation purposes and that helps in its day-to-day work. In addition, there are some preliminary materials that throw light on the results and effectiveness of volunteer work in education. For these purposes the following types of materials are appropriate: (*a*) anecdotal observations and reports by youngsters, parents, and volunteers; (*b*) reports of the classroom teacher and information contained on school referral forms; (*c*) achievement tests, especially those administered before and after tutoring with control groups; and (*d*) case studies prepared by trained observers. It should be remembered that the progress of pupils who make use of these supplementary programs should be compared not with that of pupils who are making normal progress in the public schools, but with that of the academically retarded.

a) *Anecdotal Materials.*— It is the children themselves who first produce these materials. If the emphasis is on homework, the children begin to bring their good papers to show off with great pride, and they like to display them in the center. They begin to report comments from the teachers about their progress. Report-card day is a big day: the children bring their report cards and talk about what they are working in and how they are improving. A ten-year-old predelinquent had been expelled from school several times for getting into fights and was considered by both the school and his parents to be totally uninterested in school achievement. On report-card day he walked into a center with a big smile on his face. Asked about it, he proudly announced, "You are looking at a fifth-grader." He had been promoted.

The earliest changes that are most often recorded are in the children's attitudes toward school. Since these children are known to be intelligent and working below their level of ability, this is really what study centers want most to see. Within the first few weeks the children, their teachers, and the parents often report improvement in attitude. This comes so often and so soon that it obviously represents the hopes and expectations of families and schools. It demonstrates that the center has been a real second chance for a child. The result of having someone else interested in him has also stimulated interest and hope on the part of the teacher and parents.

Parents sometimes make interesting comments about what the study center means to their children. In one instance, a mother wrote a letter to express her appreciation. She said that the greatest change was that when she and her husband came home from work, they now found the children curled up reading books. This had never happened before, and they are always surprised to come home and find the television set turned off and the children reading. Other mothers have mentioned how their children began to try to read newspapers or looked for materials to take to school because they had been stimulated to do this at the study center.

b) *Teachers' Reports and Referral Forms.* — The referral form used in student recruitment (reproduced in the Appendix, p. 119) is an effective approach for getting teachers' reports if the form is used again to solicit information about the youngster at the end of the academic year. There is no doubt that part of the value of a project is that it helps the school take a new look at a child. Even in filling out forms, teachers have to think about each child as an individual and try to define how someone might help that child.

At the end of a semester, school reports carry such comments as, "Since J. has attended the center, he has become more curious about the world around him. He has also become more eager to learn. There is improvement in composition and reading." Another teacher reported, "Reading score increased by 1.5 [one and one-half years]. Pupil's *interest* in reading has increased." Another said, "S. is more confident. He volunteers more frequently in class and is definitely more curious and interested in his surroundings. His attention span has improved greatly." Another one, asked about the change in a child, reported, "Greater interest in reading. Improved attitude towards schoolwork. A much happier pupil." Another teacher reported no change or improvement of grades or reading skills but said that "homework assignments are completed more regularly and there is an increase in attention span." Any system of evaluation is subject to hazards. Some teachers seem to lean over backwards to see improvement in order to encourage volunteer efforts. Of course, these comments are generally positive. There are also many instances in which the school does not see any change despite the child's and the staff's feeling that he is doing much better.

c) *Achievement Tests.* — In addition to reports of academic gains from the schools or from report cards, some projects administer tests to measure academic improvement. All schools do testing of children, and this information is indispensable. Sometimes the tests are out of date, or the child will not be retested at the right time for the study center's needs. Children have asked for testing in several projects and are very interested in knowing what testing is all about. They may not ever be allowed in school to see reading tests that they have taken, and this may contribute to their unrealistic ideas of their own abilities. Many of them know their reading score, but they have no idea what it is made up of or what their difficulties are.

The Gates standardized tests of reading are being used in several centers. They give a great deal of information and are not used by the local public schools. In those centers where they have been used, the children have cooperated fully. The tests were scored and given back to the volunteers as quickly as possible so that they could be shown to the children and the results explained. This has been a rewarding experience for the children because they study the tests and find their own mistakes. Often these youngsters are either hostile toward or feel defeated by testing. With careful explanation of the results, however, testing was a valuable learning experience for them which they appreciated.

The Gates tests cover a variety of different abilities such as vocabulary, speed, and comprehension; sometimes they reveal a specific problem. A number of children score low in vocabulary and do not have much knowledge of words. One twelve-year-old boy, who could recognize very few of the vocabulary words, carefully went through the whole list and then looked up to say, "I just never have come across any of these words." Vocabulary has been identified as a problem of inner city children, and this score sometimes varies from other scores by as much as a year. The low vocabulary scores in pretesting in three centers seem to reveal background deficiencies and a lack of general experience.

Another common problem is in the comprehension and the following of specific instructions. The children often have a general idea about what is needed and follow directions in general, but fail to carry through on specific details. For instance, in a test they are asked to put an X on something in one problem. In the next problem they are asked to underline something. They very often use an X in the second problem, marking the right item but with the wrong mark.

These children have an inability to stop themselves when they have reached the limit of what they know. Even on the tests that are for a specific grade level, they tend to try work that is too difficult for them. On a survey test that covers a range from third grade into high school level work, they generally try to do work that is years beyond their ability, despite careful explanation beforehand.

There is no doubt that learning to take tests is an important part of academic work. Most middle-class children learn that if you mark a lot of answers wrong, your score is marked down. If you mark something partly right, you still will get credit for that, even though you don't know the whole answer or all parts of the answer. Inner city children seem to lack testing know-how, but they are so eager to learn that it is a real challenge to help them. Since they will be taking tests not only as long as they are in school but also later on in adult life, simply teaching them something about taking tests and making a realistic judgment of what they know is worthwhile.

For a scientific evaluation, the simple design of the controlled before-and-after experiment is required. It is necessary to collect reading achievement scores, for example, on a large group of underachieving youngsters before and after the period of exposure to tutoring by volunteers. The design implies at least weekly sessions over a period of one year with a group of youngsters who are, in general, initially at least one year behind and no more than three years behind. A comparable control group of underachievers who are not exposed to volunteer help needs before-and-after testing as well.

The Illinois Institute of Technology research and demonstration project on after-school study centers is developing a research design of this variety. The work to date has been in the form of a pilot investigation designed to test out procedures and field problems. But some interesting data have been collected that indicate the effectiveness of one-to-one volunteer tutoring in raising academic performance in reading.

The pilot investigation involved testing the level of retardation in reading of a group of thirty-eight boys and girls, both Negro and white, who had been referred to a center from a nearby school. In this program the children are tutored once a week for approximately forty-five minutes. The group fell into two distinct sub-groups in terms of length of time to which they had been exposed to tutoring. There were seventeen students who had been tutored for some time — six months or more — and twenty-one who were just starting and had been tutored for two months or less. There is no reason for supposing that selective factors or special characteristics distinguished the two groups. They all had to be at least one-half year behind in reading level; in actuality, the typical deficiency was close to two years when they started. These data show that the retardation of the group that had been tutored longer was clearly smaller than that of the second group. Five children had advanced to the point where they were no longer behind, that is, they were at grade level or better. The over-all average for this group was −0.4 years behind, as compared with −1.8 years behind for the group that had been tutored for less than a two-month period.

These groups were referred by the schools through the same procedure of referral. Obviously, all students needing this type of help did not necessarily respond, but this type of selection operated for both groups. Moreover, of the group tutored longer, only two children dropped out of the program. If their retardation levels were included, the difference between the first and second group would still be marked.

These findings are only suggestive, of course, but they are most encouraging. It also needs to be pointed out that volunteer tutoring should continue for at least one year — longer than any of these students were exposed. The clearest indication of the impact of these efforts is the achievement of grade level; that is, retarded students are brought up to their proper grade level. They develop more of a sense of self-confidence. Experience to date also indicates that even after such tutoring, the stimulation that comes from continued involvement may be essential for some youngsters if they are not to fall back. This stimulation is often given in homework help to groups of youngsters who need less intensive involvement with adults.

CASE STUDIES

Generally, detailed reports are not required from tutors. In selected study centers where research is being done, however, reports by volunteers, observations by study center co-ordinators, and staff group discussions make it possible to collect case study materials on selected children. These brief accounts of children with whom tutors have worked, sometimes but not always successfully, supply insight into the problems of tutoring and of managing a study center. These materials can be used for staff discussion and training and serve as examples of the kinds of case materials that need to be collected.

JEAN

Jean was referred for tutoring by the adjustment teacher of a public school. She was a sixth-grader who was two years behind in reading. The adjustment teacher said, "Jean needs a friend." She was a heavy eleven-year-old — unattractive and generally unkempt. She had no father, and her mother, who had a very limited income, baby-sat for other people. Jean baby-sat every day with her two younger siblings and also with a little neighbor boy.

Even though Jean had been coming to the study center library for four months, she had not known that tutoring was available. She seemed quite surprised that children were being helped with reading and was very eager to have help. Jean had two tutoring lessons a week with a former teacher for approximately one-and-a-half years. At first, progress was slow, and it was hard to interest her. She was willing to do what she was told to do and read faithfully but without interest until, among the books that were offered to her, she discovered Jane Addams. This book caused the first real breakthrough in her reading; she wanted to read everything written about Jane Addams. After this, Jean was taken by her tutor to visit Hull House.

After several months of tutoring, Jean said that she would like a chance to read out loud in public school. When she was in the lower grades and the children read out loud, she was not able to do it. Now that she was able to read out loud, she was in the sixth grade and there was very little opportunity. The tutor, therefore, asked the school if Jean could be given this chance to show what she could do. It turned out to be impossible for her to have this opportunity, but the fact that she had asked was a measure of her growing self-confidence.

Although Jean liked her tutor, the most important result of the tutoring was that Jean's mother became more interested in her. The mother began, for the first time, to look for magazines and to help cut them up for a school project and to find current events in newspapers. When Jean talked about these activities with her tutor, it was obvious that they meant a great deal to her. In turn, the mother told the tutor that she had not realized before how much she had been missing by not helping Jean.

Jean developed some poise and composure which was noticed by the other people working at the center. She began to dress more neatly and to comb her hair.

Although no other book ever impressed Jean as much as Jane Addams, she continued to explore with the tutor different kinds of materials. They spent time talking together and taking imaginary trips on maps, in addition to doing academic work in reading and mathematics. Jean's world was very limited and her lessons were obviously a highlight in her life, which otherwise consisted of going to school and baby-sitting.

After about eight months, Jean's tutor started to work with another girl. The tutor began to let their lessons overlap a little, since they worked well together. Jean was more confident and talkative — the other girl, more reserved and of superior intelligence. She helped Jean with math, and in turn Jean recommended books to her. They also went on several trips with their tutor.

After one-and-a-half years of tutoring, Jean and her tutor agreed that she no longer needed this help. Although she had difficulty in spelling, she was able to achieve adequately in eighth grade. Her tutor's farewell gift to her was a small dictionary. The study center planned to have the tutor see Jean occasionally.

JIM

Jim is a twelve-year-old Negro boy who bears a scar across his cheek and a broken tooth as evidence of his toughness. He wears a dead-end kid type of hat turned backwards and walks with his hands poked firmly in his coat pockets. He is a very agile boy, interested in boxing, judo, and karate.

Jim is in fifth grade. A reading test given at school six months before he began coming to the study center showed a 3.9 reading level. A test given at the center two months after Jim began coming, during which time he was obviously not performing at his top capacity (he was extremely withdrawn and preoccupied), resulted in a score of 2.5. The school report said, "Jim achieves well in arithmetic. His achievement is otherwise poor. He needs help in listening. He seldom does homework and participates little in class."

Jim came to the center originally only to case it out and showed no interest in reading or in any academic activities. During the first week of the center's operation when routines had not been established, Jim made an attempt to steal from the center. He knew that he was seen by a staff member and returned the money. A few weeks later, a tutor's cigarette lighter disappeared. A staff member, remembering the earlier incident involving Jim, asked his help in finding the lighter. Before the evening was over, Jim had found the lighter hidden in the sock of another child. Six months later, at the time of this report, there had been no further incidents.

The study center chairman recognized Jim's leadership position with the other children as well as the potential trouble that could result if he chose to make the center his enemy. She appointed him and two of his friends assistants, giving them tasks one evening a week to aid in the operation of the center. She hoped in this way to win their support and cooperation. From Jim's aloof attitude toward everything academic in the center, it was obviously going to take time to reach him.

He liked to show off in arithmetic, in which he performed adequately. He avoided all reading activities, as though they were beneath his interest. At the same time, he came eagerly to work and wanted to help in the housekeeping duties of the center. He was unpopular because of his loud, aggressive manner.

In addition to his volunteer duties as a helper one night a week, Jim began to work with an adult one evening a week, at first as a member of his gang of four boys and later individually. (The group could not be separated at first for fear of losing them. Later they developed special interests, and they all needed so much remedial help that the staff was pleased when they were able to accept individual help.)

Jim expressed interest in working in the building trades after he finishes school. His father, who does not live with the family but who apparently sees Jim fairly frequently, works in construction. Two of Jim's older brothers also do construction work. Jim's tutor helped him build several models, emphasizing the need to follow instructions. Jim took pride in showing his finished efforts.

After two months of weekly meetings, Jim for the first time read aloud from the building instructions. The tutor began to present books for Jim to look over. One evening he read through a short, easy book and seemed pleased with his efforts.

Jim told about his report card, saying that it was mostly

"fair" except for arithmetic which was "excellent." He said, "With numbers, nothing stands between me and there," pointing to his forehead. He spent an extra evening at the center looking for information on the flags of other nations because his class was studying them in school. He was disappointed to find the only good illustrations in encyclopedias which could not be taken out of the center. A staff member suggested he take a chart from the wall, and he was very pleased. It was the first time the staff had known him to express interest in taking any materials to school.

After about twelve weekly appointments at the center, Jim reported, "My teacher says I'm doin' better and if I keep it up, I'll be almost intelligent." He told the story with great pleasure.

Jim developed a friendly relationship with both the chairman and his tutor. When the center closed for Christmas vacation, Jim and two of his friends who were building models needed one more working session to complete their projects. So that they might have them for Christmas a special meeting at the center was arranged for Jim and one of the other boys (the third was confined at home as punishment for being suspended from school). Jim was also suspended at this time but was never kept in by his parents. In time, Jim began to take an interest in safeguarding the center. Once when he discovered it had been left unlocked, he stayed on guard and sent a friend chasing after the chairman to tell her to return and lock the door.

Jim's attitude and manner have changed. Formerly a very loud and boisterous child who dominated any group situation, Jim's presence in the center became less and less apparent ever since he and his tutor started reading and building models in a small back room. He is defensive about having other children see his work. His tutor reports that he is more relaxed, more tolerant, and helpful to other children. He frequently sings under his breath as he works.

After he got in trouble at home for using bad language when his little sisters broke one of his models, the chairman suggested that he substitute the word "fudge" for the bad word. The following afternoon he came running into the center to ask the chairman, "What was that word?" She told him "fudge," and he turned to a boy who was with him and said, "You fudge-head." It continues to be his favorite epithet.

Jim is very interested in dogs, especially in the chairman's German shepherd. He recently built and painted a plastic model of a German shepherd, which he named after the chairman's dog. (He says that he owns a dog that is half Alaskan husky and half German shepherd and has recently acquired a new German shepherd pup but that someone else keeps them for him.) After he had been coming to the center for three months, he took an encyclopedia and struggled through the section describing various breeds of dogs. He did this reading silently between his tasks in assisting the chairman. He asked for help on some words and did not give up until he had satisfied himself that he had read the entire section.

Jim is a child without much parental supervision. He is apparently allowed to come and go with the only restriction that he be in by 10:00 P.M. He knows how to get around the city and travels distances by foot and by the elevated train. Twice when he and a friend were suspended from school for misbehavior, the friend was kept home for punishment, but Jim continued a very free-wheeling life. He lives farther from the center than most of the other children, but is among the most faithful in attendance.

When his mother visited the center several months after it opened to register two of Jim's younger sisters, she was told that Jim was one of the center's most frequent visitors. "Does Jim come here? Oh, that's wonderful!" He has six older brothers and several younger brothers and sisters who have a different father from Jim's. Jim's stepfather lives with the family in a small apartment in a very run-down building two doors from the elevated train. Jim's mother works, and a cousin cares for the younger children. She does not get off work until 6:30, and so Jim has a dinner of a coke and potato chips on the nights he comes to the study center.

Jim now wants to please those who have helped him. One evening after the center closed, the chairman suggested that since neither she nor Jim had eaten dinner, he join her for a hamburger. Jim removed his cap immediately upon entering the restaurant. He spoke in a low tone of voice throughout the meal. When he was taken on a tour of the restaurant by the manager, he was obviously dazzled and appreciative. The manager gave him a set of balloons that could be shaped into animals and showed him how to make a dog out of a balloon. To give something in return, Jim showed him paper and pencil tricks he had learned at the center. Jim also has been taken on field trips — a visit to the auto show and a visit to the dog show.

A change in attitude toward adults and other children, as well as toward himself, preceded any significant academic change. His experiences in the study center made it possible for him to give up some of his troublemaking. In six months of attending the center twice a week, Jim has had some work experience and has developed a stable relationship with two adults. He knows many of the staff members and now works well with a number of adults and children. Jim is different from most of the children who come to the study center, since he at first denied his need for help. For this reason the model-building and other activities were important in leading him to academic work. No one has pushed him except the other members of his gang who also started doing academic work and now taunt him that they are doing more reading. Instead of blowing up at them as he might have a few months ago, he has begun to be a bit embarrassed and says, "I'm gonna git to readin' soon."

The two adults who are responsible for Jim's acceptance and progress at the center are a young man and a young woman. One is a social worker; the other works for an insurance company. The woman who had no background in work with children did a good job in helping Jim because she genuinely liked him when most people found him unlikeable.

At the end of the academic year, Jim brought in his report card — which he says is the best he ever got. There were several "excellents" instead of the one he formerly got in arithmetic, and most grades were "good." The lowest mark was in reading, which was "fair." There were no unsatisfactory ratings, and Jim said this was the first report card he ever received that had none.

Since he has begun to read more, it is possible to see that he has special difficulty with small connecting words. He is responding to specific help with these.

STEVE

A public school referred Steve to the study center in September as a beginning sixth-grader who read at middle third-grade level. He is a middle child in a Mexican family of fifteen children. A handsome boy who was very shy, he was eleven years old but very small for his age. During his first appointment he said nothing more than "yes, ma'am" and "no, ma'am," except in answer to direct questions.

Steve was assigned to an experienced teacher for two lessons weekly. Because of his discomfort, it was suggested that he read from a book which would be easy for him so that the tutor could help him with reading. He said, "I read very slowly." The tutor told him that it did not matter. In giving him upper second-grade material, the tutor found that he read very well at that level. From his statement she had expected slow, hesitant reading; actually, he read well, although far below his ability. He was told that his reading was not slow when it was material like this, but that he would need help to bring his reading up so that his school work in sixth grade would not be so hard for him. In referring to the easy book that he read with the tutor, he said, "I never saw a book like that." The tutor mentioned that there were quite a few others and she would try to find some that he wouldn't mind reading.

Steve was asked what kind of stories he liked, and he answered, "Dog stories." Asked if he had read one he liked, he said, "No, Dr. Doolittle is the only library book I have read." The tutor suggested that this must have been hard for him, and he agreed that it took him a long, long time to read it, but that the other kids in his room helped him with his words. He was given two simple books to read at home, and it was suggested that he tell the tutor about one of them. He said, "There is not much time for reading. I like pictures." When asked if this meant TV, he said yes.

At first, Steve brought back the library books without reading them; he had "not had time." He seemed to have absolutely no interest in reading, although he liked the stories that he read during the lessons. The tutor decided that it would take some real incentive to get this boy to begin, and she made a folder called "Books I Have Read." She explained to him that he should list the books he read in this folder and that every time he finished ten books he would get a small prize. There was no visible response to this plan. He finished a book with the tutor that he had begun in the previous lesson and wrote it down as the first book. For the first time he smiled at the end of the lesson. The tutor took turns reading with Steve at first, but decided to stop because he seemed so uncomfortable.

Soon he began to ask for more books than the two he could check out on his card. By the fifth lesson he had received his first prize, which was a flashlight, but there was no reaction except suppressed pleasure. He seemed afraid to show any other emotion and sat there very controlled; he took the prize home unwrapped.

At the end of three weeks, the tutor inadvertently gave him something slightly more difficult. It was a third grade book, which was the level at which he tested, but he stumbled through it. The tutor was moved by the frustration and anger that she could feel in this boy. It was impressive to realize that Steve lived with this emotion in school every day and had done so for several years. Obviously, he could not master the work at his own grade level with his inability to read. (It was also clear that because of his intelligence, he scored higher on a reading test than the level at which he actually performed.)

When Christmas vacation came, it was assumed that his lessons would be discontinued; but he wanted to know why he couldn't come, and so he continued. His lessons were planned so that he started reading comfortably on a second grade level and reviewed third grade phonics work completely before he went on to the third grade level. He mentioned that he had had a lot of phonics in school, but the review seemed helpful.

After seven weeks of two lessons a week, all reading below second grade level was cut out, and he was able then to read beginning third grade material comfortably. In addition to general reading he began to work on exercises to improve specific abilities of comprehension. It was interesting a little later on when he was given a comprehension test. He flunked it. Two weeks later the same test was repeated in a different form, and he was allowed to read it out loud to the tutor. By doing this he scored 100.

By the end of ten weeks it was possible for the tutor to begin again taking turns in reading with Steve, since he now read well enough. They were reading books that not only were on a higher level, somewhere between third and fourth grade, but also interested him. He began to make a conscious effort to make his reading sound like the tutor's, and he looked at her and watched her very closely when she read. Steve seemed unaware of what reading is supposed to sound like or that it was supposed to make sense. When he found a word he didn't know, he tended to just pronounce anything that came to mind. When it was suggested that he think about what made sense, he immediately knew the word. There were many examples of this, and by the combination of reading exercises and free reading, he seemed more aware of what reading was all about.

Steve began to show embarrassment about the spelling in his reports. The tutor had always gone over these with him and had helped him, but now he became very self-conscious about his lack of ability. At one point, he wanted to use the word "animals" and was afraid to ask how it was spelled. Finally, after hiding his paper from the tutor for a while, he smiled broadly and announced that he had thought of another word that would do instead. He solved the problem by substituting the word "pets."

During the holidays Steve took more books to read, and he discovered a number of common folktales and fairy tales that most other children had read years ago. They were all new to him, and he enjoyed them. He read and reread one third grade book and memorized one of the stories in it because he especially liked fairy tales.

Although the school had referred Steve and given a reading score, the center had no other information on him. Nine weeks after he began his lessons the tutor visited his school. There she found that this shy boy had been a behavior problem for the last two years. He was continually banned from reading class because of his incessant talking. The tutor felt that it would be very hard for her to get him to say anything spontaneous.

After about three months of lessons, Steve's work had come up to beginning fourth grade level, and he began to read informational books instead of just nonsense books. Now there were simple history and other subject matter books from which he could benefit.

The tutor had become aware through her conferences with the school of Steve's difficult home situation. The mother had abandoned the family two years before, and this fact was kept a secret from the community. The father was afraid that if the authorities found out, the children would be taken away from him. An older sister managed the family and attended high school. As long as the mother stayed away the family managed, but after about three months of this boy's lessons, the mother suddenly began to visit. When she visited, she took some of the children out for treats and presents but completely ignored two boys, one of whom was Steve. Both boys reacted by beginning to fall apart in school, and the school became deeply concerned. At one point, Steve stopped coming to his lessons, and the tutor found out from the school that his sister had had a birthday and had been loaded down with presents by the mother. On the hunch that Steve was having a birthday, they checked the folder and found that he was. As nearly as the adjustment teacher and tutor could figure it out, he had waited thinking that his turn would come, but when his birthday came, it was ignored by the family.

After a month's absence Steve one day came walking into the center when the tutor happened to be there. (It was later learned that he had spent a week with a married sister who lives out of town. She had talked to him about school, and he had returned to school in a much happier mood.) The tutor told him she was glad to see him and then opened up his folder to begin working. He said that he hadn't done any reading lately, and she said, "That's all right, we'll just go on where we left off." The tutor told him that she was sorry she did not have his present there, because she had not expected him to come, and that she would bring it the next time. Steve's eyes filled with tears, and he tried very hard to keep from crying. He put his head down and said, "I didn't know that you knew about my birthday." He was told that it was in the school records that were given to the center. He pulled himself together with a great deal of control and began to talk about his troubles in school. The tutor was aware of these from the teacher, who had said that Steve was going to flunk unless he did some specific assignments that he had neglected all year. The main thing he had to do was a social science workbook which he had hardly begun.

The tutor told Steve about her conversation with the teacher and said that she would be willing to help him finish up this work if he wanted to do it. They began to work on his social science workbook.

Steve continued to come and worked very hard. He offered to come on holidays and weekends. After a couple of weeks it became obvious that he would need more than two lessons a week, so he began to come to the tutor's house on Saturday mornings. He spent the entire time on his social studies work. He did all of it himself but would never have done it without a great deal of help, as the material was difficult for him. The teacher was reading it to the students, knowing that many of them were poor readers, and it was amazing how much this boy got out of listening to the material read aloud. When he had to go back and fill out a workbook, however, he had no idea where to look in the book for answers. The tutor helped him find the material and read much of it to him again, since he was months behind. They sometimes took turns reading paragraphs. By working intensively for several weeks, Steve was able to finish the assigned work and was promoted to the seventh grade.

During the academic year that Steve was tutored he read and reported on eighty books of gradually increasing difficulty. But his family assumed no responsibility for his doing homework, and his school achievement was low.

Steve was out of town a great deal the following summer and

so had no lessons. When he came back in the fall, he was assigned to a man teacher in school, and the principal felt that he was doing quite well. He did not want to come back to the center, although his tutor offered to continue to help him or to ask for a man tutor for him if he preferred.

During the year that Steve did come to the center his school began after-school reading classes and he was referred to them. He refused to go. The next fall the school again began after-school reading classes and he was again assigned. He never went. Neither did he return to the study center, and the home situation apparently deteriorated. The girl who took care of the family got married and moved out, and an older brother took over. After the tutor went to the home twice, and the family pretended that they were not at home, she decided not to pursue it.

This case is presented as one of our failures, despite the academic gain made by Steve. The age of the boy and the deteriorating home situation made it impossible to really succeed. We did help Steve more than we helped any of the other referrals who were as old and as academically retarded. Greater success, however, has come with those children who are younger and less retarded in school achievement.

George

George's grandmother was referred to the center by the parochial school in the community. George was eight years old and was repeating first grade. He could read only a few words.

In the first interview, the grandmother told the director of tutoring that George had been with his mother until he was five years old. She had neglected and physically mistreated him, so he was taken away from her and custody given to the father. George then came to live with the grandmother and the father. The grandmother talked about how difficult it was for her to take on a child and kept repeating that it was like having another baby, since George didn't even know how to keep himself clean. As there was no kindergarten at George's school and the grandmother was working, she sent him to a day-care center. He was picked up at six in the morning and brought home after six o'clock at night. She did not know what the children did there besides color with crayons.

The grandmother had a desk, blackboard, and books for George, and she tried very hard to teach him herself but felt that she could not do it. His father also worked with him but was very short tempered.

In March, George was assigned to a tutor, a housewife who was taking teacher training in a nearby teachers' college. He was brought to and from his appointments by a neighbor boy who was slightly older and who baby-sat with him after school. (George could not come by himself, although he lived near the center. It was several months before he was trusted to cross streets by himself.) This boy was mean to George and continually called him stupid. Whenever George had a message or anything to carry home, the boy would insist upon taking it because "George can't remember anything." The staff refused to accept this and tried to encourage George by handing him the material or putting it into his own pocket.

George had apparently had no prereading experience. He was given reading-readiness materials and taught to differentiate between symbols. There was no evidence that he had ever been taught anything academic except memorizing a few words. He did not know his colors or the basic concepts of size and shape. He did not know his street address or phone number, the days of the week, or the months of the year, and he could not count to ten. He could write a few numbers, all backwards.

The tutor who first saw George was unable to continue after six lessons. By that time it was near the end of the school year. George's grandmother came to talk to us several times; she was grateful for the help he was getting but, of course, was impatient with him.

Several things happened with the coming of summer. The staff members had had enough opportunity to talk to the grandmother so that when she brought up the question of the boy taking care of George, they were able to add their observations, which agreed with hers, that this situation was unsatisfactory. The staff encouraged her to send George to day camp, and she did so. This meant that George could not have lessons during the week. The school had given him a couple of basic assignments to complete during the summer. If he could finish reading a certain primer and count to one hundred, they would promote him to second grade.

Temporary help was given to George during the summer by a tutor who was an experienced teacher and saw him once a week. At first, it was very discouraging. The only bright spot was that he remembered what his former tutor had taught him. He had memorized the first part of the primer that the school assigned.

George still had a very short attention span and was very discouraged. He would put his head down on the table and act as if it was all too much effort. After a couple of weeks of summer day camp, his attitude changed. He sat up and talked spontaneously for the first time about "my club" and what he did there. He was out of town part of the summer and only had six lessons, plus help from the grandmother who asked for and accepted supervision in helping him. He finished the school assignments and learned a little more basic information — for example, weekdays in sequence. He learned some number concepts and could count and write the numbers in sequence to 100.

George's grandmother was given suggestions for activities to carry on with him, including a Dot-to-Dot book, so that he would not forget his numbers. The new tutor in the fall was offered the same suggestion. It turned out that George had done so many of these during the summer that he was tired of them, and they were much too easy for him.

In the fall, George was promoted to second grade in school and assigned a regular tutor every Saturday morning. (This tutor had no teaching experience but was prepared to work with him for a period which lasted two years.) He did not attend regularly during the winter, but improved in the spring. The father explained that the boy was subject to upset stomachs and light colds, and that was why he missed.

It was a problem to work with the grandmother. Her inclination was to be very hard on George and to treat him as a dummy. She told us once that they had decided to be very strict with him because he was disobedient. When told that he was also very frightened, she seemed surprised. It was explained that he read with a question mark in his voice after every word because he was so unsure, and that unless he gained some confidence in himself, he would not even try.

Another problem was her concern that there was no program for herself. Twice she mentioned that she wished there was a study center for her, and when told how well George was doing in day camp, she said, "I just wish there was something like that for me." She was told that the center wished, too, that it had more programs, but that there was help for adults at a local high school. She asked about it twice, at the same time telling the staff that she was too old and too busy. In April, however, she said that after her talks with the staff, she had returned to night school to finish high school. She had not wanted to say anything until she was sure she would graduate. She did graduate in June.

George mastered a sight vocabulary and began to sound out words. He acquired a fund of knowledge that other children his age already knew. The staff noticed his visible gains in self-assurance. The most important change, the tutor felt, was that his family no longer treated him as if he were dumb. He began to relate to other children and was superior in some games. He assumed a gentle, but definite leadership in showing other children how to play the games he had learned.

In summary, George did kindergarten work during his first semester of tutoring and, after a year, had completed first grade and functioned at an early second grade level. He was by no means ready for third grade, to which he was promoted, and his lessons continued.

George again attended day camp the following summer and in high spirits resumed his lessons the next fall. He had the same tutor as before and also the same teacher at school, who was appreciative of his progress at the center. When asked about school, George said that it was fine. "What was the best part?" He grinned and said reading.

MARION

Marion's parents brought her to the center after they had read about it in the community newspaper. Marion is one of five children in a Negro family who lives some distance from the study center. She was an honor student through the fourth grade, and then her grades began to go down. Now, at twelve years of age, she was flunking seventh grade. The parents had tried for two years to find some help for her. The last two summers they tried to get her into summer school, but the school told them that Marion was too capable and openings must be saved for the many children who were not able to work up to their ability. The school felt that because of superior intelligence, Marion was perfectly able to do the work if she wanted to.

The mother said that Marion spent from 4:30 to 10:30 every night doing her homework and never finished. The parents had tried everything. When asked to name some of the things they had tried, they named all punitive measures. The mother was practically in tears, and the father seemed to feel quite desperate. They had investigated a reading clinic and had found that it would cost two hundred dollars, which they could not afford.

Marion had an older brother who was an honor student. She refused any help from him, and the mother felt that her own education was so inferior that she could not help. The father, who was able to help, was not home very much. It was pointed out that it would be difficult for a girl to have a brother only one year older who does so much better in school. When it was suggested that, of course, they were very careful about comparing the children, the father said sincerely, "We haven't been at all careful about that. We do it all the time. I'm sure that's part of the trouble."

An experienced tutor was available and was asked to spend a little time with Marion while another staff member talked to the parents. The tutor felt that the girl was so extremely capable that she could certainly be helped. It was decided that Marion would come to the center until a new center near her home was available and that she would transfer there. The solution to one problem seemed to be to offer her a place to do her homework away from the home, where the mother stood over her and the child never finished anything.

The tutor worked with Marion for five months. At first, Marion brought stacks of homework and seemed at a loss where to begin. She had a great many ideas about how to do her assignments but had trouble getting down to work. The tutor encouraged her to talk over possibilities and then at some point just to begin. Marion was soon able to finish all of her homework assignments in the hour-and-a-half that she spent at the center. She had a forty-five minute appointment with the tutor and then would stay and finish up afterwards.

Marion was extremely shy and unsure of herself. The first real excitement came when the tutor gave her two tickets to a neighborhood play. Marion talked excitedly about how much it had meant to her to sit with an integrated audience and watch an integrated group of performers.

The tutor had to go away for a couple of weeks after a few lessons, but encouraged Marion to come in and use the center anyway. The staff doubted that she would come because of her shyness. They were all very pleased when she came and accepted homework help from other adults.

The center that opened near her home was never available to children of Marion's age, and she therefore continued with us. She was promoted in school and then set herself a very ambitious summer program. During the summer she continued to see the tutor twice a week. Together they worked out the subjects which were of particular concern to Marion. These included spelling, English, history, math, and book reports. She was provided with materials and assignments, but the structuring of her lessons included help from her. She made herself a schedule and decided to work every morning for an hour-and-a-half.

During the summer Marion learned to have realistic expectations about her own ability. At first, she was too ambitious in what she planned to do each morning, but then she learned how much she could do in that length of time. She worked faithfully on these subjects through the summer and received, through her tutor, a scholarship at the YMCA. In addition, she and the tutor made several trips around the city.

Through the book reports that she wrote and illustrated for the tutor, Marion began to develop an interest in art. She began to talk about people outside the center, particularly a Japanese girl who was her seatmate in public school. This girl taught Marion perspective in drawing, and Marion gave her hints about drawing.

At the present time Marion is completing her homework, doing well in school, and developing some of her interests in art. She set up an art project for herself and will call the tutor when it is finished. The tutor is convinced that Marion has some real ability in art and is trying to get an art scholarship for her so that she can get further training. She and the tutor agree that she no longer needs tutoring.

According to the tutor, the biggest change in the life of this girl is the reaction of the parents. Their original complaint that "Marion doesn't care about anything" is no longer true. Marion now cares a great deal about success in school and is doing so well that the parents are supportive and talk about how proud they are of her.

Donna

Donna was referred by the neighborhood parochial school when she was in the sixth grade. She was tutored once a week in arithmetic and reading skills. In addition to her one appointment weekly, Donna often came for homework help. The main impression of Donna was her lack of general information and experience. She also had no confidence in herself and talked with a slight stutter. Originally, the school asked that she be helped with arithmetic. Watching Donna solve written problems, the tutor realized that she also needed help with reading skills, particularly comprehension.

Reading-workbook activities and small specific assignments gave Donna experience in following directions and completing work. She gradually learned to work by herself. At first, she needed continuous support and encouragement, and when left to work alone after the teacher went on to work with another child, Donna would leave the study center. She gradually gained confidence in herself and in her ability and was able to continue working alone after her regular appointment had ended. The tutor found specific weak points that they worked on. One day, after four weeks of individual instruction, Donna was excited to find that *m* and *n* were separate letters of the alphabet. She had thought that *mn* was one and the same letter.

By the following summer, Donna had become friendly with several adults at the study center. Her stuttering had disappeared, since it seemed to be no more than an expression of her shyness. When the summer program began, Donna was an active participant. She joined a reading group for children of her own age. Their activities included speech and art work which Donna enjoyed. In addition to participation in this group, the staff accepted her as a helper with the younger children, realizing that she also made use of the help that these children were getting.

By the middle of the summer, Donna became one of the three teen-age girls who worked half-time as volunteers at the study center. The center had become aware of the lack of general experience and knowledge in Donna's life. During that summer the staff learned that she did not have any books of her own, not even a dictionary. She was helping to repair some old ones, picked out a discarded book, and asked if she could fix it up for herself. After that, staff workers made a point of locating other books that they could give her for her own library.

Donna's tutor left for the summer just at the time the center was offered a scholarship with an experienced remedial reading teacher. This woman, who gave private lessons at home, baked and gave the children snacks when they arrived. The staff decided that this would be a pleasant experience for Donna, not only because she still needed tutoring in reading, but also because of the social experience. Donna enjoyed this. Once a week she had a lesson with this teacher, who gave the center reports on her work and continued using the same materials that Donna's former tutor had used. In addition, Donna came to the study center in the mornings and worked as a volunteer.

By fall, the remedial reading teacher felt that Donna was doing quite well and that she should not continue the long walk to the tutor's house. Donna therefore began to come in for general homework help. She said that school was going well. She mentioned a couple of times how pleased the teacher was with her academic progress.

Donna is one of our more successful graduates, but the benefits the center gave here were only partly academic. The academic help in reading and arithmetic was crucial in helping her to do well at the eighth grade level. This help, however, was supplemented with a great deal of social experience and with broadening of her academic background through books. The center may even have helped her explore her future ambitions. During the summer that she worked so faithfully as a volunteer and showed real ability in working with young children, a staff member asked her if she had ever considered teaching. She said, "No, I think I'll be a secretary." She was assured that that was a fine choice of a career. Later, during the year that Donna came to the center only for homework help, she told one of the women who helped her several times, "I am thinking now about being a teacher."

The center's favorite memory of Donna will always be of her choosing simple reading books to read "to the little kids." After selecting four or five and very excitedly talking about the stories she had previously never heard about (such as that of the Bremertown Musicians), Donna would then proceed to gather a group of small children around her and read to them. It was hard to tell who enjoyed it more, Donna or the little kids. Moreover, the reading out loud and the growth in self-assurance of this formerly shy girl probably meant as much to her in her personal development as the academic help. The fact that the staff could give her both explains their success.

<h2 style="text-align:center">JUAN</h2>

Juan was an eleven-year-old fourth-grader who was small for his age. He was born in Puerto Rico and came to the United States before starting school. He attended first and second grades in several different cities of the United States and had to repeat second grade. Then his family returned to Puerto Rico, where Juan attended third grade. They moved to Chicago the following year, and Juan entered fourth grade.

Juan had failed the fourth grade when a new study center opened across the street from his home. A social worker had tried unsuccessfully to interest the parents in allowing the children to attend recreational groups. A study center volunteer, Carol, tried to encourage Juan and his sisters to attend the study center. They said their parents would not permit them to come. After Carol visited Juan's mother and found that she did not speak English, she returned at a time when his father was home to translate. Although his father can speak English well enough to be understood, neither parent reads in English.

Juan's father owns a small store, which Juan's mother operates during the day while the father holds another job. After he gets off work he relieves his wife and runs the store in the evening hours. Many household tasks fall to the children who must go home directly after school to clean the house.

Carol found that Juan's parents were opposed to their children having contact with Negro children in the community. This distrust was reflected in the children, who did not play in the neighborhood and who later revealed to the study center staff their fear of "the coloreds." When the purposes of the study center were explained to Juan's parents, they were very willing for their children to participate once a week. The father voiced his concern about Juan's two failures in school. When the center later moved to a new facility three blocks away, it was necessary to make another personal visit and arrange for the children to be escorted to and from the center. Permission to increase the lessons to twice a week was given after the father saw that Juan was progressing.

The necessity to learn to read in two different languages had confused Juan so that he had less reading skill than a first-grader. His school reading score of 2.7 was inaccurate, since he was unable to read in a first grade book. He did not know the sounds or the names of any of the letters of the alphabet. He had a small sight vocabulary and had memorized the words in a reader. His only tool to attack an unknown word was guessing.

Extremely lacking in self-confidence, he was very quick to tell anyone who inquired about his grade, "I flunked twice." His teacher reported: "Juan is a very strange, withdrawn child. He seems to be afraid all the time. Very often he will not answer a question or talk at *all* when I ask him something. He bites his nails and sucks his fingers all day."

Carol decided that Juan needed self-confidence as much as he needed to learn basic reading skills. Because he memorized easily, they worked on rote learning at first, combining drill on phonics with study of Juan's spelling list for school. After a few lessons, he received a grade of 100 on a spelling test. This was the first 100 Juan had ever made. As his tutor continued to devote some time to spelling, he continued to make 100's.

The tutor continued to stress phonics. After three months of two lessons a week Juan's tutor, Carol, who is a student at a local teachers' college, began to see him four days a week. The lessons included work in a special set of readers and his school reading text. Juan now studies his spelling independently and continues to make 100's. He has also begun to make 100's in arithmetic and brings in several papers weekly to show to his tutor and other staff members. Juan's father bought him a special plastic briefcase to keep his papers with 100's in. Several of his papers are on display on the study center bulletin board.

After approximately forty tutoring sessions, Juan is reading with relative ease in a middle third-grade reader. He had been in the lowest reading group at school, working on a second grade reader. Recently the other children in this reading group were put back from fourth to third grade, and Juan was advanced to the next reading group. He was very proud of the fact that he was the only one from his former reading group to remain in fourth grade.

Juan had once told his tutor that his teacher was mean and that she yelled at him when he made mistakes. Recently when his sister mentioned that Juan had a mean teacher, Juan corrected her, saying, "She used to be, but she isn't mean anymore," indicating that possibly the teacher's attitude toward him changed.

Juan often shows his tutor how he has sounded out words that occur in the text they are reading and tells her that when he reads in school, he sounds out words. Phonics has given him confidence in his ability to read words accurately, and he likes to demonstrate his ability and to recall occasions when he has received compliments from his teacher for using this new skill.

Juan's mother was concerned that his recent report card showed no improvement at all, despite his obvious progress. She asked the tutor to accompany her to school, and they talked with Juan's teacher. The teacher said that although his report card did not improve, he would be promoted to fifth grade.

Without the study center, Juan might still be sucking his fingers and biting his nails. He would probably have flunked for the third time.

Appendix

STUDENT REFERRAL FORM

N_____ P_____ Study Center
School Referral and Follow-Up Form

Date_____

Child's name_____ Address_____

Age_____ Date of birth_____ Grade_____ Phone_____

Teacher's name_____ School_____

What is the child's reading score?_____ Date of test_____

If arithmetic is a problem, what is the score?_____Date of test_____

Over-all academic performance. Good_____ Average_____ Poor_____

In which subjects is he strong?_____

In which subjects is he weak?_____

What is the child's attitude toward school? For example, how much self-confidence does he have in his class performance? Does he participate much in class? How much interest and curiosity does he show?

How regularly does he complete homework assignments?

How is his attention span?

Comments, suggestions:

THANK YOU

Bibliographic Note

Among the standard materials that our centers use most consistently are the phonics workbooks *Building Reading Skills* published by McCormick-Mathers Publishing Company, Wichita, Kansas. The *Reading for Meaning* workbooks, Lippincott Company, Philadelphia and New York, and the Reader's Digest *Skill Builders* are also extensively used. The *Structural Reading Series* published by L. W. Singer Company of Chicago has been very successful in individual tutoring. Kenworthy Service (John Green, 411 West 6th Street, Covington, Kentucky) has a wide selection of reading and arithmetic activities. Some of these materials are available at school supply stores. *Reading Aids through the Grades* published by Teachers College, Columbia University, New York, is a helpful source of ideas for remedial activities.

Among background materials that volunteers find helpful, *The Culturally Deprived Child* by Frank Riessman, Harper & Row, New York (1962), is most widely used. Sylvia Ashton-Warner's books, *Spinster* (1958) and *Teacher* (1963), Simon and Schuster, Inc., New York or Bantam Paperback, dramatize the value of individualizing instruction. Her approach reflects the technique developed for New Zealand teachers working with Maori children.

Education and Income by Patricia Sexton, The Viking Press, New York (1961), presents the basic inequality of American schools. James Conant's *Slums and Suburbs*, McGraw-Hill, New York (1961), is another exposition of this problem.

Educational work with culturally deprived children means creating a social and personal setting in which youngsters are supported in their efforts to explore the world around them and develop a sense of identity. The experiences of working with emotionally disturbd children are relevant for understanding the interpersonal problems involved in dealing with children who feel defeated and frustrated. Bruno Bettelheim's *Love Is Not Enough*, Free Press of Glencoe, New York (1950), supplies an overview of these problems.

Acknowledgments

In my work with volunteers in education during the last three years, I have had the cooperation of a number of public and private agencies. Dr. Curtis Melnick, Superintendent of District 14, Chicago Public Schools, has been most helpful since the inception of study centers and tutoring projects. The Hyde Park Neighborhood Club, under the executive directorship of John Ramey, operates a study center in which I worked with volunteers and youngsters. I have also had effective cooperation from the South Shore YMCA Study Center, in which Mrs. Kurt Neustaetter serves as community co-ordinator. Mrs. Alyce Evans, Director of McKinley House, helped to develop a center there. Officials from the Chicago Housing Authority with whom I have cooperated include Claude Miller, Mrs. Dorothy Morrison, and Wendell L. Johnson.

In Chicago, city-wide support and co-ordination of volunteer tutoring and after-school study centers is supplied by the Committee on New Residents of the Commission on Human Relations, of which Edward Marciniak is director. John Hobgood, the Reverend Daniel Overmyer, and Albert Logan are staff members with whom I have worked closely. For the State of Illinois, the Governor's Committee on Literacy and Learning, with Joyce Bollinger as co-ordinator, serves a similar function.

Our demonstration and evaluation project is supported by a cooperative research grant from the U.S. Office of Education (No. G-027). Dean Hans Mauksch of the Illinois Institute of Technology is responsible for the administration of this project which has made possible demonstration centers at McKinley House, Douglas Study Center, and North Park Study Center. Dolores Long is project co-ordinator.

Index